Are You Worth It?

Liz Almond

Second Edition

Herkimer Publishing

Are You Worth It? Business Edition

Copyright © 2015, Liz Almond. All rights reserved.

First paperback edition printed 2016 in the United Kingdom

Second paperback edition printed 2017 in the United Kingdom

ISBN 978-1-910815-04-5

A catalogue record for this book is available from the British Library.

Published by Herkimer Publishing

www.herkimerpublishing.com

Cover design by Clair Melville-Brown/CMB Designs

'The Love Game' © 2015, Liz Almond. Design by Clair Melville-Brown/CMB Designs

Other images included in this publication are used with permission. Copyright remains with the original owners.

Printed in the United Kingdom

This book is dedicated to all business owners and entrepreneurs in the business community. Whether you realise it or not, you are all healers. Your product or service is reducing stress for your customers and allowing them to feel good which in essence is helping them to be happier and more relaxed. By recognising your own self worth and by valuing yourself, you will continue to stay in business by making the money you deserve and therefore you will heal more people. Thank you for playing your part in reducing the impact of depression in the world and I wish you every success in staying empowered, inspired and happy whilst helping those around you.

The fantastic book course I attended by Sharon Lynn and Lorenzo Guescini inspired and guided me to successfully write this book and thankfully I was sponsored by Rosemary Williams, Business Coach at a time when I could not afford to do the course.

"Liz's book helps me to understand my thoughts around money and gives practical solutions to make changes - finances are a vital part of business and relationships. Plan to succeed, plan time to read." - Rosemary Williams, Business Coach

Thank you Rosemary for believing in me x

Rosemary Williams, Business Coach
Connect on LinkedIn • Visit my website: rwcoaching.co.uk
Find me on Facebook.com/rwcoaching • Twitter RWCKent

"I shine a light on your current business situation, helping you resolve issues which hold you back. You'll enjoy lightbulb moments as you step out of the fog, and forge ahead with greater clarity."

Amazon Customer Reviews

for

Are you worth it? A Spiritual Guide to Managing Your Money Mindset for Business Owners

"I purchased this book & read over a 2 day period I literally couldn't put it down. So many aspects to the book touched me on so many levels. It's given me so much practical & spiritual advice to get me to where I want to be in my business. I feel I know what to do & feel comforted in knowing I'm not alone with my fear on numbers. It's so well written & easy to understand. It's come to me at a perfect time." **Karen Jones**

"This book explains exactly how to manage your mindset around money, Liz has approached this book in a friendly, personal, insightful manner. She explains in great detail how to change negative thought processes to clear the way for abundance in your life." **Mel Smith**

"Are you worth it? This is the simple question Liz asks and the answer is of course I am. We should celebrate our successes and work on our challenges. If money is your issue, Liz can help you change your mindset. An excellent read with a powerful and inspiring back story." **Donna Law**

"This book has helped me so much on my path of self awareness that I always have it to hand. Superb book written by an author with obvious life experiences." **Daniel Bodle**

"A very useful and encouraging book for business owners and non business owners alike in helping to re-establish positivity, self worth and direction in life. Full of useful tips and exercises, the book follows a logical progression to help in long term goal setting as well as in day to day life." **Neil D'Silva**

Foreword

LIZ AND I MET in 2013 as business contacts. As a financial adviser and working in a very facts and figures world, I didn't understand nor believe what Liz was telling me about what she did for her clients. Reiki and her other mindset skills seemed hocus pocus, but I thought it was wonderful as it was helping people in a positive way.

Around this time, I agreed to do some skill swapping with Liz to understand each other's businesses more. What came from that was me taking my business to the next level. I went from stalling (although I didn't know it) to deciding I was going to take action and start recruiting new team members. Liz has gone on to be there to provide me support in times of rough waters and calmed my thoughts. How? I have no idea. I cannot even go on to explain how.

What is amazing about Liz, is all the time in helping myself and many others, she was going through such a massive troubling time herself. This book I see as not only a tool for her to share her knowledge with more people but also to prove to herself that she has overcome her own difficult times and life is now is such a positive and fruitful place.

I will be giving this book to my clients as a gift and I believe it will change their mindset about money.

Rebecca Robertson

Evolution for Women, Financial Planning for Women and founder of Evolving Women in Business

www.evolutionforwomen.co.uk

www.financialplanningforwomen.co.uk

www.evolvingwomeninbusiness.co.uk

Acknowledgements

I would like to thank so many people who have helped me to create this book as well as those who have given me such support when I really was at my lowest. I feel deep gratitude towards all those people who have helped me. I am extremely lucky to still be alive and seeing the richness in life once again. Whilst I could not possibly list everyone, there are specific people I would like to recognise.

- ♥ My wonderful family - My late Mum, Dad, John, Helen, Kate, Allan and co. You have been so generous and caring. Thank you from the bottom of my heart. Dr Liz Lurring for encouraging me, believing in me and introducing me to holistic therapy. It is now time for me to take over from you. Bidde Dimond, thank you so much for your love and support.

- ♥ Dean Almond - thank you for the happy times and for ensuring I took on board the wealth lessons of life.

- ♥ My friends - Hayley File and Wendy and Derek Eagle. Thank you for being there for me when I needed you most.

- ♥ My neighbours - Judy and Gary Millen, Diana and Michael Beaman, Jacqui Harris Jones and Susie and Tim Brooks. Thank you for all your help.

- ♥ Laura Luntrau and family - my wonderful, Romanian lodger and family for making me giggle and raising my spirits when I was in dire need.

- ♥ Ash and Sarah Lawrence, Richard Taylor, Maureen Johnson, Rosemary Williams, Scott Johnson and other members of the ABC Network who took me under their wings and spurred me on gently.

- ♥ Rebecca Robertson and all the wonderful Evo Girls for accepting and loving me.

- ❤ The members of my Millionaire Mindset Course - Gareth Powell, Simon Pollard, Sally Marshall, Paul Williams, Adam Loynds, Neil D'Silva, Paul Douglas, David Shaw, and Lloyd Lundie. Thank you for your advice, support and encouragement.

- ❤ Chris Verbiest for fixing my laptop when I could not afford to pay and for gifting me with another one. You are an angel Chris.

- ❤ Gareth Powell for being a great friend and for filming me several times only to find that we couldn't use the content. Your patience has been really appreciated.

- ❤ Ben Wells for helping me to sell my jewellery when I couldn't pay the mortgage.

- ❤ The therapists who have helped with my recovery and to refocus me - Sonia Hurren, Penny Tree, Sarah Christie, Andrea Beadle, Trisha Wood, Jad Orlinksa, Peter Vaghan, Lindsey Agness, Paula Barham, Margaret West, Karen Bashford, Caroleann Block, Sharon Cresswell, Fraz Smith, Paula Doyle, Sarah Johnson, Sara O'Donnell and Caroline Hart. Thank you also to Catherine Watkin - for being so encouraging, supportive and for teaching me to be a receiver.

- ❤ The accountants who are putting me on the right track to success and how to understand money in business - Morena Russell and Andy Springett.

- ❤ Clair Melville-Brown for the fantastic book cover and for bringing to life my design of the love game.

- ❤ Sharon Lynn and Lorenzo Guescini for a fabulous book course which gave me the knowledge to get this book published.

Contents

Introduction

I'VE HAD AN EXTRAORDINARY and privileged life but for some reason, I've had some very faulty and negative thought patterns which have created ill health in me, caused me to get into massive debt and at one point in 2014, I came very close to ending my life as I was extremely unhappy, felt out of control and could not see another way out despite the very in depth psychological training I have had.

I'm very happy to report that I have now turned my life around and the lessons I have learnt and the wisdom I want to pass on to the world is within this book. I do not wish anyone else to ever have to experience what I have been through and it is my great pleasure to pass on my deep spiritual wisdom and knowledge about health, wealth and happiness in life. At the core of everything was a lack of self worth and it is my wish to inspire, empower and enlighten through this book for you to know that 'You are worth it and are enough!' Life is a gift and it is a blessing to be alive.

My story is that I was born with anxiety, an unexpected twin with a heart defect. I was a very sensitive soul and I still am. I've spent a lifetime, comparing myself to others, trying to be a perfectionist and being very judgemental which was largely down to the anxiety I had from interacting with others. I was reacting to life and those around me, rather than learning from each experience and making choices which were non judgemental, win-win and solution focused. I didn't love myself. As a deeply sensitive Cancerian, I do go up and down emotionally, get easily hurt and I have now accepted that I go up and down with the lunar phases linked to the new and full moon.

Having started off my working career in the hospitality industry, an accident in 1996, literally changed my life. I developed Chronic Pain Syndrome and I did not work for 2 years. I became depressed. I was predicted by doctors to only have 70% of my function for life. I was introduced to the world of holistic therapies at this point by my sister's godmother, Dr Liz Lurring and my interest in holistic medicine started at this point. Whilst I had had hundreds of doctor and consultant appointments and had reached the end of the line in conventional medicine, not one person suggested that maybe I was creating my bad fortune myself and it was my thought patterns that had to change.

I can tell you now, I created the ill health and unhappiness I suffered. Not consciously, but unconsciously as I did not know any better at the time. Even the accidents I had had in my life were a pattern. Every time I had had an accident, it was at a point in my life that I was not happy and I changed careers. I had learnt as a child that if I hurt myself, I would get more attention. Clearly I was not doing this consciously and this belief underpinned the accidents I was having. Strange but true....

The health lessons in life

Following receiving a Reiki 1 empowerment in 1998, within six weeks I was off benefit, returned to work as an IT Lecturer and trained to be a teacher. Without doubt the Reiki empowerment I received, changed my life and allowed me to reconnect as a person and to become more confident. My life started to change for the better. I was still in lots of pain but determined to succeed regardless.

In 2003, I trained to be a professional coach as well as a Reiki Practitioner. Within eight years, I was working full time as Teaching and Learning Manager at a large college, managing the lesson observation system for 500 staff, reporting on quality systems as well as managing a coaching service which supported lecturers to improve their teaching performance. So much for only having 70% function for life. According to Department of Health statistics, most people who are off work for more than six months, never return to work. This is a travesty. This is usually because they have lost their confidence after six months, and are given insufficient support and training to help them to work on their thought patterns and behaviour to change their lives and circumstances. The support given is mainly practical support such as CV writing, interview skills, work experience, etc.

In 2010, I had massive change in my life and this is when I realised that I had been creating lots of negative experiences from my thoughts and behaviour. I was already a professional coach at this point and I decided to learn Neuro Linguistic Programming, Hypnotherapy, Time Line Therapy, Cognitive Behavioural Therapy and Emotional Freedom Technique to Master Practitioner level. I released so much emotional baggage from my past and could see how my negative thinking had impacted my life. I now had the wisdom to be a Reiki Master Teacher.

I was opened up to the realisation that my thoughts and behaviour were actually creating my pain and what I was experiencing in life was of my creation. My self awareness was heightened! I noticed my health improve massively as I let go of the past emotionally and reduced the anxiety I had been feeling. I haven't taken any pain medication since 2004. I've learnt lots about my health during this time and realised that there are four aspects to my health which I must take care of - spiritual, mental, physical and emotional health.

The wealth lessons in life

So how did I get into so much financial trouble? I had never been in debt until I started my business in 2011, even when I was a student or on benefit, I had had money. In this year I unfortunately experienced a miscarriage at 13 weeks. I was devastated. I'd never been particularly maternal, but I had begun to accept and be happy that I was 'good enough' to be a mother. During this time, the college I was working at was experiencing a big restructure, and I helped everyone else around me to accept the changes and to be ok about moving jobs or leaving the college. I didn't look after myself enough. As I was not allowed to use my new holistic skills on staff and did not feel valued by my employer, I decided to take voluntary redundancy and start my business Insightful Minds. I really did not appreciate how lonely and lost I would feel as a new business owner and also had not appreciated the loss I would have had from leaving my work colleagues.

As I turned 40 in 2011, this was the last time I could have IVF on the NHS, so regardless of bad timing, I then had two failed cycles of IVF in the hope of having a child. Without a doubt, I was becoming depressed and was diagnosed with high blood pressure. To top it off, I started off as an Educational Consultant in business, but I just couldn't get it working. I now realise I was really naïve about business and how to stay in business. In my therapy room, I was getting all different types of clients - with depression, exhaustion, phobias, health issues, etc. I had such a big skillset and I didn't know what to focus on. What was my niche? Let alone my microniche!

I confused those around me including my husband, family, friends and my network, as I was confused as well as depressed. I didn't realise that I was meant to be healing others through other healers. I didn't know that my target market were business owners and I was instead going after consumers. My self worth was at an all time low. I had gone from knowing exactly what I was doing in a successful, well paid senior management position as a leading teacher trainer and being in total control to a being a business owner feeling inadequate, insecure, and out of control.

By the end of 2011, my redundancy money had disappeared. It hadn't been spent on anything frivolous. I wasn't however wise to how I should manage money within a business i.e. tracking expenses, outgoings, etc as I was quite number blind and therefore avoided any numerical jobs in my business. Maths has always been an issue for me. It wasn't a problem when I was employed as I had a set amount of money coming in each month but with both business and personal outgoings to pay, I found this very stressful. I also didn't know how to network effectively and had no strategy to what I was trying to achieve.

The first debt on a credit card was a holiday in Egypt in January 2012. My husband thought his business would have cleared what we spent, but sadly it didn't. To make matters worse, he got sick with pneumonia whilst away and it was not a good holiday. Within weeks of him recovering, my parents were involved in a serious car crash and after ten days my mother died. In the same week, I had to have my beloved cat, Samurai put to sleep too. The next year, my sister in law died too. Multiple bereavements in such a short space of time were very hard to cope with. I sank deeper and deeper into depression.

Over time with not understanding the management of money, mixed with fear and shame, the debts kept racking up. Things just got out of control. There was such a black cloud around me. It wasn't clear how an intelligent lady like myself had got herself into such a mess. I tried to find any work, just to have some money coming in. I couldn't find anything, probably because I was just too desperate. I was being helped by friends and family, but I still couldn't get things under control. I was so ashamed and although I would ask my husband for help with managing the finances, it never happened. I think he found it difficult to talk about it too.

The lack of communication between us became worse and worse. I think because we both were feeling worthless and depressed. I was at my wits end. My husband became more and more distant, not understanding or supporting what I did as my career. He didn't understand networking and was telling me it was a cult. In April 2014, he decided he needed to leave me. I was devastated. He was my world. This was the final nail in the coffin and I came very close to ending everything. The shame of not being able to make my business work and then my marriage failing was just too much to take.

All the way through this horrible period, I've been applying what I learnt from my psychological training. The techniques and knowledge in this book have helped me to recover my wealth once more. They will do the same for you too if you are finding it a challenge to make the money you desire or can't see your way out of debt. The key really is about being positive, having a vision, valuing yourself and others.

The happiness lessons in life

I've been through so much in life and have been so lucky to meet many wonderful people along the way and to learn and experience so many things. It really has been an extraordinary life so far. By going through it, it has given me the wisdom to pass onto the business owners I work with, so that they can also heal themselves and be strong and wise for their clients. Life events impact your results in your business and it is important to take action to help you regain your health at these times. I now have a multi award winning business and I am proud and happy to say I am having a great life.

Happiness is a choice. Feeling 'I'll be happy when…. I have a new car, new boyfriend, new house…..' does not work. Happiness is within the moment of now. You have to live in the present. If you aren't feeling happy now, you are almost certainly trapped by negative emotions linked to your past or fear for the future. By applying the information and techniques in this book, you will be empowered, inspired and energised to see a new world out there. One which you create.

Love yourself and others and be grateful for everything you have in life. You only have one life and now is the time to appreciate it. By focussing on your love for life and others, just notice how much more wealthy and rich you are. It is not just about how much money is in your bank account. By being happy and feeling good, you can manifest anything you want into your life. By changing any faulty money beliefs, you can earn more money. What do you desire? Plan how you are going to get what you want and go for it!

I really hope that you gain wisdom and success from reading my book. I am deeply grateful that you have purchased it and it is my greatest wish that it empowers and enlightens you to amazing health, wealth and happiness as you heal yourself by taking part with the exercises in this book. Please pass the book on to anyone you know would benefit especially those with depression. Now is the time to invest in you. I would recommend that you buy a journal to accompany this book or download the one which accompanies this book and complete all the exercises to get the best results. Modelling other successful people cuts the learning process by 50%, therefore the book contains expert advice from money gurus to help you achieve your money goals extracted from the top books about abundance.

With love and gratitude

Liz Almond, The Healer's Healer

(1)

Are you living an abundant or scarcity life?

'Destiny is not a matter of chance, it is a matter of choice.'
William Jennings

I T IS MY WISH that those reading this book are inspired, motivated and empowered to take charge of their finances, their emotional state and their thinking, so that they can beat depression, ill health and negative thinking around money naturally.

I've had depression on and off throughout my life and whilst I have always looked for a natural way to recover, it has meant that I have had to learn massively about myself, become very self aware about just how sensitive a soul I am and change my behaviour to get different results about my health, wealth and happiness. It is not been an easy road, it has been very challenging and it is my desire to teach you some of the techniques I have used to change my life and my finances, so that you may learn from my mistakes and have an easier route to enlightenment than I did. Your business will go from strength to strength as you apply the techniques within this book.

The outcomes of this book are that you will be able to:

- ❤ Appreciate how your thoughts are impacting your health, wealth and happiness

♥ Make friends with money and understand your current financial situation

♥ Change your existing thought and behaviour patterns towards money

♥ Be clear and specific on how much money you wish to attract

♥ Take inspired action on all opportunities that come your way

♥ Change what you expect to receive and in essence receive more money

♥ Lift your emotional state, reduce anxiety and see the richness of life

♥ Declutter your home, car, office and garden to attract more money

♥ Follow your passion, do what you really love doing and you will attract more money

♥ Stay connected to your truth and you'll stay connected to abundance

According to the World Health Organisation by 2020, depression will be the 2nd biggest disability in the world. Cancer will affect 1 in 2 people. It is time for change. Mental health (mindset) needs to be treated more seriously and this book is an essential read for any business owner who is feeling less empowered and happy than they would like.

A spiritual approach to life, allows you to see your health holistically. We are all individuals and when we understand our spiritual path in life and understand our purpose, we can then create the life we desire including as much money as we want. Living our life with passion. We can also learn to heal ourselves if we choose to. I clearly suffered from highs and lows in life and reacted badly to life as I was so sensitive to those around me and my environment. Was I depressed? Yes and the changes I have made have been achieved naturally and without medication.

This book is aimed at business owners but essentially the advice within it will help anyone.

Money is such an emotive subject. Some people have it, some people have lots of it and some people have none. Some people love having it, some people hate having it, some people are jealous that other people have it and they don't. Some people judge people for being wealthy or poor. Others really don't care. The more you don't take responsibility in life and blame others, the more this will affect your overall wealth and health! Had you realised this is the case before now?

As I was growing up, my parents worked really hard as teachers to provide, however money was not plentiful and often as a child I felt poor. At primary school, my best friend lived a few doors away and I used to envy her as whatever she wanted, she was bought by either her grandparents or her Mum. If she ever needed money, it was given to her. I have to admit, I even stole money from my parents as I was so desperate to fit in and to keep up with her. Looking back, I now realise that I was deeply jealous of my friend and what she had.

On reflection, she was being bought things to mask the emotional issues around her parents separating and the fact that as a single parent, her Mum had to work long shifts as a nurse to survive. My friend had to live during the week with her grandparents and would only see her Mum at weekends. I wasn't grateful for the fact that both my parents were at home and whilst we didn't necessarily have all the material things my friend had, I had a secure family home and we had plenty of fun experiences and happiness.

My parents watched their pennies and I was programmed into thinking that money was scarce as a family and you couldn't have what you wanted. I now realise this was untrue. I must point out that my parents did not deliberately intend this, but subconsciously I took on beliefs that I must worry about money and I was also hampered by negative experiences around maths and finances, which made me feel bad. When I was eight, my twin sister was lucky enough to have a fabulous maths teacher called Mr Mars who was really fun. Unfortunately, I had Mrs Minehead, who was very strict and who made me feel very anxious. I was even physically sick over a maths exam and this emotional event stayed with me until only a few years ago, when I realised that it was hampering my success around money and numbers still.

This emotional event was behind me failing my Maths O level, and I almost failed both my BTEC National and Honours degree because of the Accounts units! Numbers are just not my thing! This has caused me so much anxiety and when I lost thousands of pounds whilst being in business, I can now see how my anxiety and lack of understanding of managing the 'numbers' in business were linked to my self worth as well as not understanding how to create financial projections for my business. If you have had a bad experience of maths in the past, this may well be hampering your success and is one of the issues I work with when with 1-1 clients. There were other emotional factors for me as mentioned at the start of the book which affected me too and you may be the same.

Whilst this is no sob story, I have come to realise how many people get themselves into financial difficulty due to emotional issues and in the worst case scenario, suicide is taken to escape the embarrassment and fear of being in debt. I want to change this situation and help those around me to understand that if you look after your health, have the correct money beliefs and you are willing to change your behaviour and how you are feeling, the world is your oyster.

The bottom line is that everyone has the same possibilities of making money than everyone else. It is a choice and it is also about becoming self aware about how you are reacting to your interaction around money and to other people around you.

I've had many ups and downs around money in my life and this is one of the reasons why I am able to share what I have learnt from my individual journey with my quest for being healthy, wealthy and happy. What I have learnt is that my health is my wealth. I've also discovered that 'being rich' can be interpreted in a very different way to the physical sensation of having a lot of money in the bank. I've had a range of jobs - some well paid, some poorly paid and I've also been on state benefit. The amount of money I had depended on the choices I made in life which were often the wrong choices depending on how I felt at the time. The more you focus on sorting out your health and wellbeing and maintain the right money beliefs and behaviours, your wealth will flow and your happiness will follow.

Having regained my health, wealth and happiness naturally, I want to inspire people who are reading my book or attending my workshops to know that they can change things too. It is my wish to help those who find themselves in some form of adversity - ill health, poverty, homelessness, debt and/or even those struggling to succeed financially in business, that there is another way. I am a very lucky lady having overcome major adversity. I've done it by having a winning combination of support and therapy, bringing together medicine, mindset and energy.

I now realise and am happy to admit that I created that adversity from my thought processes and now that I am much more self aware and have the right techniques to change things, I am healthier, wealthier and happier as well as much wiser. Now you might be thinking why on earth would you put yourself through a load of negative things in life like accidents and ill health, but I was doing most of it unconsciously and I promise you I was not aware of my negative limiting beliefs which were holding me back. I was living from a scarcity mindset and was not loving myself. I believed that there was never enough of what I needed, and therefore I was never satisfied.

One of my biggest learnings in life is about being positive and relaxed. I spent the first 35 years of my life as a very negative person and had no idea how I was coming across to other people. What I know now, is that the more that I thought negatively, the more my health suffered and so did my bank balance. My negative, scarcity thinking was linked to depression and anxiety. I had very dysfunctional thought processes and programming.

Your thoughts are creating either a scarcity or abundant life

According to Marie Claire Carlyle, who wrote the fabulous book 'How to be a money magnet in 21 days', whether you realise it or not, your thoughts and everything you touch is energy. If you have a negative thought or worry, this affects how you feel and behave and your energy is affected. According to Albert Einstein and research carried out in Quantum Physics, everything that we see, hear and touch is all made up from energy, even solid objects and our bodies. Our thoughts are threads of energy which are giving out a particular vibration or 'vibe'. The vibration is either 'positive' or 'negative'. Everything is connected, so a persistent thought will have a definite impact on its surroundings.

There is a definite need for positive 'vibes' as the better you feel within and the more you love and accept yourself, the more health, wealth and happiness will flow into your life. Your inner wealth attracts your 'outer wealth' and how you are seen by other people. The happier you feel, the more self worth you have. The higher your 'vibe' or self worth, the easier it is to manifest what you want in life and attract what you want by the Law of Attraction. Find out more about the Law of Attraction in Chapter 4.

When you recognise how your thinking is affecting your ability to make money and your health, amazing things will start to happen in your life:

- ♥ You will experience less stress

- ♥ You will have more energy. In fact the more energy you have, the more money you will have provided you have set yourself financial targets to reach

- ♥ More positive things will happen in your life, naturally

- ♥ Your focus will be more about bringing happiness to others which in turn will bring you more happiness

- ♥ Your spiritual purpose/mission will be much clearer

- ♥ Your health will improve

- ♥ You will focus on what are the most important things in life to you, the things which make you the happiest

The problem is, when you have no money, you tend to focus on what you don't have and worry about not having money to pay bills, etc. The more anxious you are, the more subconsciously you are pushing away, the very thing you are wanting! That is the Law of Attraction in action. Start thinking more positively about money and focussing on abundance and you will become healthier, happier and wealthier. You have to attract what you want by feeling good and appreciating what you already have.

So here is why:

When it comes to gaining financial freedom, the mind works from two different places - Abundance or Scarcity.

So which one are you living from - abundance or scarcity?

Cast your mind back to your childhood. How were your parents when it came to their finances? Were they ever anxious around you when it came to money or did they regularly review their finances, budget, save money and talk as if money was always ok? As you grew up, did there always seem to be money to do what you wanted or was there always a struggle or shortage and this meant you could not have or do what you wanted as there was no money available.

Scarcity

If your parents were anxious about money, they would have been living from a scarcity mindset i.e. there is never enough money and there is always a struggle to survive and to ensure there is enough money to pay for everything which is needed.

People who live from this mindset are also conditioned to believe that there are limits to what can be earned based on their money beliefs. They are generally not grateful enough for what they have in life. Often they close down to opportunities and are focused on just finding the money to pay the bills rather than seeing the bigger picture and knowing they are good enough to earn what they want. Some common behaviours are not looking at their finances on a regular basis, worrying about money, not saving as there is never enough to do this and buying items to gain instant gratification to feel better.

If you do have a business, how are you feeling at the moment? Are you living from scarcity? How is this impacting your business?

Abundance

If however your parents reviewed their finances and budgeted, and saw life as a world of opportunity to make money - they would be living from an abundant mindset. i.e. they believe they would always have enough money to do whatever they wanted to do in life. They believed that the world provided an abundance of opportunities and resources to have wealth readily available. They believe that wealth comes to you in many forms - love, good health, peace, nature, joy, and prosperity. You would be much more likely not to worry about money and will have taken on their behaviours such as budgeting and saving and not being worried about money. They are grateful for everything that they have.

So, as you grew up, you were programmed to think like your parents (all behaviour is learned) and also other influences such as school and church would have conditioned you as to what you thought about money as our beliefs about money and lots of other things in life are set up in our neurology from the time we are born up to the age of 7-8 years old. There is a continuum of time in the mind and you are able to access memories from the past to gain information. If you have negative emotions attached to these memories, for example 'I must worry about money', you will find that there are some lessons to learn around these memories to allow you to detach from the past and to change how you are interacting around money. When I work with my 1-1 clients, I help them to release these negative emotions, to help their vibe to go up and become more positive.

Your path in life.....what are you creating?

Have you ever looked at your past in detail and noticed the patterns in your life? When I say 'your past', these are the significant events, positive and negative in your past, since you were born until now. When I did this for the first time, it was a bit of an eye opener! I hadn't consciously realised how many accidents I had had. When each accident had happened, this then lead into being off sick for a period of time. Each time, I had had an accident, I had not been happy in my life. What I hadn't realised until then was that I had changed careers each time. My money was affected too. I find most people are living in the past, where as they actually need to live in the present 'the here and now.'

When I do this process with my clients, they often have patterns playing out too such as feeling unsettled due to moving house many times, many bouts of ill health, repetitive episodes of behaviour e.g. feeling isolated, or angry at others. There is so much to learn when you look at your past, as your past is showing your spiritual path so far.

By looking at your life this way, you are seeing your life in a holistic way i.e. taking in all elements of how you are interacting in life. If you don't like what you see, then make a decision to do things differently to gain better health, wealth and happiness. Look closely at what people told you about money in the past and now. Do you tell yourself that items are 'expensive'

Exercise:

How is money affecting your life now? Be honest with yourself. What is really going on? How well are you managing your money at home and in your business? Are you able to save anything? Are you spending any money on yourself? What are you having to sacrifice? Is everything a struggle? Do you openly talk about your finances with your partner? If not, why not?

So if you could have abundant rather than scarcity mindset - what would it look like and how would you have to be to get it?

or you say to yourself regularly 'I can't afford that!' If you find yourself doing this, then it is time to change. You can always change what you say in your mind to something more positive. You have a choice. You can always say 'how will I be able to afford this?' and take action to earn the money.

A simple way to reprogram the negative thoughts is to wear a rubber band on your wrist. Every time you say something negative to yourself, ping the rubber band. The pang of pain is your reminder to change! If you are regularly confirming to yourself that you can't afford something, then guess what, you will never be able to afford it!

I love working with clients on a 1-1 basis as I can analyse their past in detail for them to find out specifically what they need to work on to ensure they become happier and healthier quicker. I always find out more about them than when they do it alone. You will discover a lot from doing this exercise yourself though, which is why I am sharing it in this book.

Another fascinating element of looking at your spiritual path in this way is that you can assess the health issues you have had in the past and what you currently have, which allows you to look at your holistic health. Your holistic health is separated into four elements spiritual, mental, physical and emotional. They are all interlinked.

In 1984, Louise Hay, an inspirational healer wrote a book 'You can heal your life' as she had realised from working with her clients that their thought processes were creating health issues and discussed how positivity could overcome the health issues being experienced. Latest scientific research is showing that by changing your thoughts, your health can improve. This is backed up by many patients who have overcome health issues such as myself.

Unfortunately the fact that we have recovered isn't necessarily on record with the doctors, so it does not show up as evidence for researchers to know that patients have got better due to using other complementary therapy techniques. For anyone who would like a more scientific explanation of

Exercise:

Write down your life history (your spiritual path) - positive and negative events in chronological order. What patterns can you see? What are you repeating? What emotions are you expressing? What limiting beliefs do you have? What behaviours do you need to change? If you could have anything in your life right now what would you want? What do you currently have that you no longer want? What do you not have that you now want?

what is going on, I would suggest you read the books of Dr David Hamilton. His book 'Is your life mapped out?' is a fascinating read.

Anyone trained in energy medicine/holistic therapies such as Homeopathy, Acupuncture, Reiki, Emotional Freedom Technique, and Kinesiology will look at the body differently to the pure medical approach. Everyone's body has seven main chakras (energy centres) which spin and each is linked to an aspect of your life. These chakras get blocked and spin either too fast or too slow which means that the related aspect of your life will be affected. For example, if you had difficulty in communicating in different situations such as meetings or when you are meeting someone new, you may find that the throat chakra gets blocked. You start coughing, clearing your throat, etc.

The chakra which is related to money is the sacral chakra. It is also related to sex, power and creativity. When I work with clients, there is often an issue with money and if I delve a bit deeper with them, they often divulge that they haven't had sex for a long time or there is a problem linked to something that has happened to them sexually that they did not enjoy in the past. Worst case scenario is when rape or abuse has been present. I was raped and this caused a block with all my intimate relationships around trust and being able to fully enjoy the sexual experience with my partners including my husband. All these issues can be overcome, and this allows money to flow once more as soon as the chakra is unblocked.

Another common health problem when there is a financial issue is lower back pain. Louise Hay states that the probable cause is fear of money or lack of financial support. When a person is not trusting the process of life, they will feel insecure and their self worth will be affected. The limiting beliefs a person has around money will cause them to be anxious e.g. worrying about how to pay the bills or giving off negative 'vibes' and this will push away money from them. The anxiety is often felt around the stomach area and if it is more extreme, the person may experience symptoms such as an upset tummy or irritable bowel syndrome.

To attract money in, you have to fully trust that the Universe will provide for you. When I work with clients on this problem, I specifically work on the emotions of anxiety, distrust and insecurity. Then we look at how they are interacting around money. Often clients are just looking for money to pay the bills and focussing on a lack of money rather than focussing on their happiness. Also they are not focussing on the amount of money they need including profit to earn and are not target driven.

A really common pattern, is that someone is doing a job which they do not love which makes them feel less energised and happy. They are doing it for the money, rather than because they are passionate about it. To make the most money, you need to be working doing what you love instead. This will then give you purpose and you will in turn make more money as you will devote the time and energy needed to put the best into your work.

If you are a business owner, often the problem is that your mind is still interacting around you being employed (i.e. you receive a secure amount of money each month), rather than adjusting to a flow of money which goes up and down. In business, you have to project what you earn and put in place targets to achieve, which link to your business plan and vision board. It takes a while to feel secure with the fact that money comes from different sources at different times rather from one source on a particular date!

According to Sally Marshall in her book 'Delegate2Elevate - 7 steps to success for sole traders', the first step to success is to explore your vision and then to look at how to make your vision a reality. Without a vision, and high self worth, you will find it hard to get off the starting blocks with your business or you will jump too far ahead and then realise too late that you need to rewind and go back to what your vision is, especially when you are trying to work out what your niche or micro niche is.

Your spiritual path will be indicating to you about what your vision should be and often you do need coaching or another person's perspective such as a mentor like myself to help you see what you are unclear about. Your spiritual path will often indicate your ideal clients too as you can see from your journey in life what you can make easier for your clients from your knowledge and experience.

You can waste a lot of time and money on things in your business such as your advertising, web site, promotional materials, and networking when you don't have a clear vision. I certainly did and therefore I always advise caution to any new business owner. It is all in the planning and looking at what you really want in your lifestyle as well as what money you need to achieve it. Focus on a micro niche, something specific that other business owners understand and you will be referred work e.g. bridal hairdresser, or a therapist specialising in Fibromyalgia.

Making money is simple. The four fundamental things to do to manifest money according to Rhonda Byrne from inspirational book and film 'The Secret' are:

- ♥ Think more thoughts in a day of abundance than a lack of money

- ♥ Be happy now, without the money

- ♥ Be truly grateful for everything you have now

- ♥ Give the best of yourself to others

According to Ester and Jerry Hicks, in their insightful book 'Ask and it is given', you need to make a clear decision to focus solely on feeling good. If you are not feeling happy, you have to focus on getting the happy feelings back, to raise your vibe and to help you manifest money more easily.

It is also important to acknowledge the influence of Feng Shui. Whilst, I am not a Feng Shui Master, I am intuitive and I can often pick up issues around someone's home or office or place of work which is keeping them in scarcity. For example, as I approach a person's house, the front is very telling. If it is covered in weeds, litter is on the floor and the house is not looking cared for, then it is indicative that there are other problems going on in the house. When something is not being appreciated and looked after, then the person owning the property is not being abundant and is probably not looking after themselves too. They could use the excuse that they don't have the money to 'fix up' the house, but often simple things such as cleaning, painting, decluttering and weeding are minimal cost.

By taking this time to 'love' the property and to change the environment, the house will feel more loved and energised and will attract new energy into the property. Even cutting down high hedges will allow more energy to flow. This in turn will give the people living there a more positive environment to live in, which will make them feel happier. By feeling happier, they will be able to achieve more including earning more money. There is also a finance 'zone' in your house. If money is not readily available to you, identify the most cluttered part of your house and start decluttering it. Sell, recycle and give to charity what you can to clear this space. The best time to do this is leading up to a New or Full Moon.

How does everyone's mind work - neurological levels

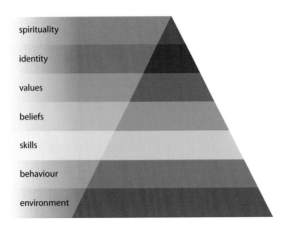

Robert Dilts - Neurological Levels
Ownership of image: www.pinterest.com/pin/180777372512764946/

This can then be related to Robert Dilts model of neurological levels in the mind where if you work on the environmental issues affecting a person (the lowest level), someone's neurology will shift for the better provided you have improved the environment! Every human being has different levels within their minds which eventually lead to spirituality. When I empower a client to Reiki, I am working high up on this pyramid, as the empowerment will enable a person to become more self aware. I also work on their mindset too as if they have an energy shift, they also need to consciously know what to change in their behaviour too to get different results.

When it comes to money, often it is the values and beliefs that get in the way of achieving what you truly desire. You may have faulty or limiting beliefs which are sabotaging your success. As a person becomes more in alignment with themselves, they will understand their identity and why they are on the planet. Anyone can make as much money as they want, if they want. It really isn't greedy unless they keep all the money for themselves.

For example, if they have always believed that someone like them can't make money (they may have come from a very poor family), then this will sabotage their success. They will need to be taught how to believe something different and how to achieve it. They may need to be taught new skills too such as money management or how to use the internet or stock market to be able to make money. Anything is possible.

The more you work towards being the true you, the authentic you, the more lighter and brighter you will become. This is why personal development is so important for business owners as otherwise you will stagnate and not achieve your full potential. If you don't keep learning and you become too fixed in your mindset e.g. too many black and white thoughts linked to stubbornness, your body will start to respond in the same way and your health will be affected. Remember energy is supposed to flow and be flexible, so flexible thinking is key to your success.

As soon as your health is affected, the profits in your business will be affected. By learning about yourself, in the search for enlightenment, you will uncover so much more beauty in your life, by overcoming challenges and by becoming so much more resilient. Patience is a spiritual virtue which you have to learn. Sometimes we are going too fast through life and by becoming more mindful, you can appreciate the time you have. When we are annoyed about something, this is an indicator of a lack of patience. Pay attention to when you are feeling annoyed about something as you need to change this behaviour.

Throughout your life, you would have been responding to the neurological levels (within your mind) as you stepped along your spiritual path of your life, you just probably hadn't realised it until now. When someone is searching for their purpose, it is because the mind is focussing you this way. As soon as you decide to start a business your whole energy system will be shifted as you have to stand on your own two feet, with full responsibility for everything that happens within your business. There is no one to blame or to take responsibility for you and money will not just arrive on a set date like it used to when you were employed.

You therefore have to take your own personal development very seriously. If you don't develop yourself whilst you have a business, your business will go bust especially if you don't resolve your lack of maths ability. Abdicating your accounts to your accountant or bookkeeper is not acceptable. Overcome the anxiety, learn how to be happy around numbers and work as a team with your financial experts. You need to learn to step outside your comfort zone and to take calculated risks.

When you aren't sure what you are meant to do in life, you can feel your life has no purpose or vision, and this is when you can lose hope, which de-energises you. You will feel more tired and frustrated and this will of course affect your ability to make money in your business. As you will find out in the Love Game in a later chapter, you can go against the flow without a purpose and vision for what you want in your life or you go with the flow, living life on purpose with a vision. If you have had one or many bereavements seek out help from a therapist such as myself. It will give you strength and will help you to manage this time more effectively and to help minimise the impact on your business.

According to Sunil Bali, 'Happiness, fulfilment and even enlightenment come from having wonderful relationships where you're not afraid to be wrong, have no ego and have a burning desire to be of service.' This means that you have to change how you are thinking when you are communicating with others to get the best results. You may well have to change your behaviour and learn new skills such as Reiki or Neuro Linguistic Programming to get even better results.

According to Laughter and Life Coach, Caroline Hart, 'Success is having time for yourself and others and enjoying the moments you are blessed with. That is true success.' This is so true. Often I find my clients are so focussed on money or the lack of money, that they miss the true essence of life and what it is all about. They often feel that they will be successful when they have money and chase the money so much that they miss out on life. They just work harder and harder to keep up. Feeling good and successful now, will bring you success, not feeling that you will be successful when you have earnt a certain amount of money. By feeling good, you will attract more opportunities to earn more money!

What is mindset?

To succeed and to have a profitable business, it is important for you to understand the importance of having the right mindset in business. If your mindset is not focused and you are living too much 'in your mind', you will find it more difficult to build a successful business. Your money mindset will influence your happiness.

Your mindset links to your own personal qualities such as your intelligence and talent and how your mind is working. You may be good at having a focused mind or might be quite scatty and live 'in' your mind too much. You may over analyse everything or you might just go with the flow and give issues in your life little thought. You might be a very floaty 'spiritual' person and be very ungrounded which means you miss some of the practical elements you need to complete, to achieve things in life or you might have your feet firmly on the floor as you like to see evidence before you make a decision which means that you procrastinate and don't take action as you are worried that you might make the wrong decision.

Someone who has a fixed mindset, believes that their destiny is pre-determined and that what they think and how things are is how things are meant to be. They think life happens to them and not that they create it. They do not realise that they need to be flexible with their thinking and they have a lot of black and white thoughts, often caused by being stubborn and by not moving out of their comfort zone. Someone who has a fixed mindset is not willing to understand or admit that they are holding onto limiting beliefs (or decisions that they made in the past) which are stopping them from achieving things in the here and now. They do not believe that they have control to change aspects of their life.

Someone with a growth mindset however, is much more flexible about their thinking and knows that they can change a circumstance or issue by changing their thinking in an instant. They may do this by reacting differently to a situation or by thinking differently and visualising another more positive outcome. You always want to have a growth mindset, to be flexible with your thinking and always to act as a learner in your life. Learn from situations and set intentions for how you would like things to be in your life. Using a positive mindset and visioning towards success in your business or life is key.

Mindset stands for:

M   Mental Health

I   Intuition

N   Nourish

D   Decisions (limiting)

S   Senses

E   Emotions

T   Thoughts

Mental Health

Keeping your mental health in check is vital to you having a positive mindset. Mental health has been massively misunderstood in the past and has been given a negative perception due to this misunderstanding. You do have control of your own mind and you can direct it to think how you want it to think, but you need to re-programme it and deliberately change your thoughts. Your mental health directly relates to the thoughts that you say to yourself in your mind. If you are thinking negatively, you will feel negative and therefore get a negative result from thinking this way which will potentially affect your finances. Your mind is very powerful and by overanalysing situations, you can escalate a problem or issue which causes us to react negatively in our behaviour and to feel bad.

In Cognitive Behavioural Therapy, there are 13 different thinking types such as catastrophising, personalising, magnifying, black and white thinking, etc where we make situations worse by our thinking. By analysing our behaviour, our thoughts and our reactions and asking ourselves how we could change things so that we feel better, allows us to let go of negative emotions which we are feeling and to release issues from our past.

Your mental health is directly linked to your spiritual path i.e. the journey you have been on through your life. If you have had multiple negative experiences such as abuse, parents splitting up, rape, bullying, divorce, relationship breakdowns, homelessness, etc, these will all affect your mental health and how you are feeling. As these are all negative experiences, you will feel negative unless you deliberately start to see a more positive point of view. This can be achieved through practising gratitude, forgiveness and releasing the negative emotion in your body which is making you feel bad.

Later in this book, I discuss the TEAR model – Thoughts, Emotions, Actions and Results. Your thoughts come first as these create your emotions, which affects your actions and results. Whether you like it or not, you are creating these negative experiences and reactions, and the plus side is that you can change your thinking and create a much better life. Releasing the negatives, will help you manage your mental health more positively and help you feel more grounded, balanced and happy.

Intuition

Following your intuition is key and often people say trust your gut instinct or gut feeling. This feeling is linked to your solar plexus chakra and is our energetic way of sensing if something feels right or wrong for us. Our academic system sadly does not allow us to use our intuition effectively and we are often taught that you need to 'evidence' what you know without trusting your own judgement and using discernment. Learning to trust your intuition is key to your success. As you sense something feels right in your gut, you will make decisions in your mind about how to feel, act and behave in a situation.

Your intuition is your inner guidance system and it is wise to follow what you feel instinctively. The more you trust this, the more you will get in tune with what is right or wrong for you. When you are really 'in tune' with yourself, you can use methods such as body dowsing to give you 'yes' and 'no' answers to your questions. I often use this method if I have a decision to make or just want to check what feels right for me without overthinking a situation. The more you trust your intuition, the more you will get in flow with your life and what is right for you. It is important though that you release any 'trust' issues that you have, otherwise your intuition will be coloured by these negative experiences in the past and you may be more judgemental than you need to be about people and situations.

Nourish

Nourish your mind by taking time out to clear it. You can do this by sitting quietly and meditating. When you have a full mind, you will get overwhelmed, forget things and will have a more stressful time. You need to learn mindfulness meditation techniques which allow you to 'switch off' your mind rather than it being on the go 24/7. If you are always in the 'doing' rather than 'being' mode, your mind will be constantly active which is exhausting. It will also affect you being able to sleep properly. By nourishing your mind, you will be able to live with a more positive mindset. Nourish your mind by feeding it positive affirmations, powerful information about how to change it to be more effective and take time to clear it several times a day.

Different ways to nourish your mind might be to listen to music, to walk through the countryside, to sit and listen to the sound of the waves by the seaside or to do an activity such as making cards, drawing, creating raw chocolate or reading a fiction book which does not stimulate your thinking.

Look after your mind. It is creating everything which is happening in your life and in the future. Your thoughts create your life, through the Law of Attraction. It does need to be kept active but also have times of rest too which will give you the right balance.

It is important also to put your needs first. Your happiness must always be number one. This is not a selfish thing to do. You will have more energy to help others if you do. This way you are honouring and nourishing your soul and it's needs.

Decisions (limiting)

Decisions which you made to yourself in the past (whether in this lifetime or not) are affecting you right now unless you decide to change them. The decisions you made in the past are potentially limiting you and are therefore limiting beliefs. For example, you may have been influenced by your parents who were war babies. They said to you as a child, you must eat everything on your plate always so that food is not wasted. You then take this on as your belief. As you grow older, you are struggling with your weight, but you still feel you must finish everything on your plate, and you just can't sense in your body when you are full.

By removing the limiting decision of 'if I don't eat everything, it is a waste', you will then be able to get in tune with how much you actually need to eat and will stop eating so much. This belief can be changed by you deciding to change it or you may need professional intervention in helping you to release it.

The decisions you made in your past about money and the management of money are colouring what you are receiving right now in your life financially. It is your job to listen to your thoughts in your mind and to work out what beliefs are you holding true about life. Any negative beliefs need to be changed so that you can have a more positive life and experience around health, wealth and happiness.

Senses

You are sensing everything through your five senses – sight (visual), sound (auditory), touch/feeling (kinaesthetic), smell (olfactory) and taste (gustatory). As you can see from the picture, when an external event happens to you, your mind goes through sensing the experience. Your mind filters things through these experiences.

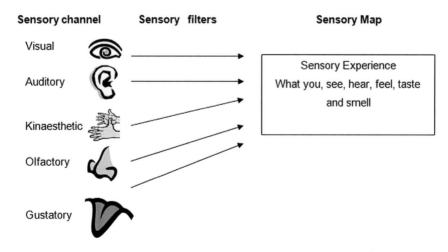

Ownership of image:

http://www.nlpacademy.co.uk/articles/view/making_sense_of_the_world_nlp/

For example, you are at a book launch. You are taking in visually everything at the book launch such as the cake, the book display, the banners, the people there etc (sight). There may be music playing which links with the book's theme (sound). You may be meeting people you know and you are feeling happy or you are feeling nervous as you realise you know no one (touch/feeling). There is a scent of lavender in the air as the book is about aromatherapy (smell) and as you bite into a piece of cake, your mouth is flooded with the taste of lemon which is your favourite (taste). You will create a memory in your mind which is either positive or negative about the event.

In Neuro Linguistic Programming, the picture you create of the memory in your mind is called an internal representation. As indicated in the picture below, as a person experiences an external event, it goes through their senses initially and then the person filters this through their mind by deleting, distorting or generalising the experience as well as other information which makes up their personality and what they believe in and value. This final picture or internal representation which they create in their minds may be very distorted to what actually happened at an event.

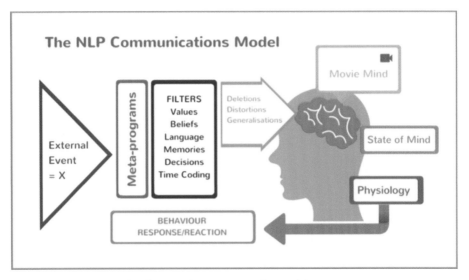

Ownership of Image: https://www.thecoachingroom.com.au

The more negative the internal representation is, the more it affects a person's state of mind, their physiology and their behaviour. When the events are very negative that someone experiences such as abuse, violence, accidents, disasters, divorce, someone close dying, redundancy, etc, the many internal representations the mind holds on to can be just too much and a person will block events to try to feel better. Sadly, the mind will still reference to these events until the person has therapy or learns to releases the negative emotion in some way.

The positive and negative memory is now a picture in your mind which links to the senses you went through. We create these pictures about all our experiences in life and they build up in our mind along a timeline which we cannot visually see except in our mind. Your mind will reference to these experiences when it is trying to decide whether to do something for the future. For example, as a child you saw a spider in the bath and you were really scared. You will have seen the spider, possibly heard it scuttle along the bath trying to get out and you will have felt fear. Every time you see a spider in the future, you reference again to this first time you saw the spider and those feelings of fear and the fear builds in the body.

By keep feeling the fear and linking it to spiders, you then set up a phobia of spiders. This fear feels very real and will stop you from doing other things in your life as the emotion of fear is building in your body from the root cause of seeing the spider. If you are fearful of making a sale in your business, this adds to the original fear of the spider as the emotion building has a cumulative effect in the body over time. By removing the phobia of spiders and the emotion of fear from the body, you will no longer see fear in the same way as FEAR actually stands for False Evidence Appearing Real as our minds 'create' issues which are not really real.

As we reference to the pictures in our mind, this links to how we feel. The great thing is though is that these pictures can be changed in the mind, so that you feel better. The emotions can also be removed or reduced. This can be done by using therapy techniques such as Neuro Linguistic Programming, Emotional Freedom Technique and Reiki.

Another way our senses might affect us is when we are thinking and smelling at the same time. You might be thinking about a specific person when cleaning a rug and thinking that they are getting up your nose and irritating you. You sense something in your nose (a tickle or smell) and you link what you are thinking to cleaning the rug and the dust coming off it.

Logically, you think you have an allergy, but actually it is because you are thinking about an experience when someone irritated you. It is always worth paying attention to what you are saying to yourself when you are not feeling well too as often the language that we say in our minds or even out aloud is indicating that we have a problem.

We sense each other around us constantly as we are in each other's auras (the energy field around the person). We can pick up things unconsciously about the people who we are with and when you are in rapport with them and the other person is relaxed. You may well pick up how they are feeling that day and lots more as well such as what they are thinking about.

Obviously when seeing another person, we can feel their energy too and know if they are happy or sad from how they look if we pay attention. You may ask someone, 'how are you today?' and they say 'not bad.' We know from what they are saying and how they look that life is not as great as it could be, as they would have said 'brilliant thanks!' if it was and would look happier.

Finally, it has also to be noted that some people are more highly sensitive than others. They may feel different to everyone else, as if they don't fit in and they are picking up on other people's emotions and issues and don't know how to tell others about why they are able to pick up on the pain or suffering of others. They may pick up on seeing things around people like auras or say that they can see spirits or guides. They may hear noises or feel things when they go into rooms. They may feel a bit weird and others may tell them that it is not true what they are sensing as only they can see/hear/feel it.

If they are not believed, they may isolate themselves as they find it difficult to connect with others. This happens to both children and adults. I attract this sort of person to work with me as in my world, weird is normal and the person just needs to accept themselves as normal, not different.

Emotional Health

Emotions (feelings) go up and down in the body and are either positive or negative in how they feel. If you are like me, you may be deeply empathic which can be the reason why you struggle with handling your emotions and how you feel. In the mind, you either think in pictures, sounds, touch/feelings or logic. If your lead type is touch/feelings, you may be actually able to feel other people's pain and suffering. You may not realise that you tap into this and take on board their negative feelings and pain to help them and in a bid to relieve their suffering. Some people can also see and feel the pain of others by looking within another person's aura (magnetic field around them).

The problem with this behaviour and how it affects your mindset, is that you are always putting someone else ahead of yourself which is not a good thing to do. You must always put your happiness first and understand that everyone is responsible for their own issues and they must motivate themselves to love themselves enough to make changes in their life to improve their health, wealth and happiness. If you are taking away their pain for them, they are unable to learn the lessons they need to learn about looking after themselves and around the fact that your health is your wealth.

If you take on board another person's stuff and you have your own issues too which you have not resolved, you can then overload your body with too many negative emotions such as guilt, fear, anxiety, anger, etc which will lead your body to becoming toxic and ill at ease and you will potentially create chronic disease such as cancer, fibromyalgia, chronic fatigue/pain syndrome or ME within yourself. If you would like further understanding of how you might be taking on board other people's emotions and how they link to ill health, I would be happy to have a complimentary chat with you.

Take responsibility only for how you are feeling and what you are saying to yourself in your mind. What you are saying creates your mindset and by learning techniques such as meditation, Reiki, Emotional Freedom Technique and Neuro Linguistic Programming, you will be able to raise your vibration and to feel more positive.

Thoughts

Your thoughts are very, very powerful. They are literally directing your life. You need to be monitoring them at all times, paying attention to how you feel in different situations. For example, you may go to a network meeting and you just feel anxious. You don't know people and you aren't sure how to network. You can feel your confidence levels dropping as everyone seems to know everyone and what they are doing.

By thinking this way, you are putting yourself into a negative mindset which will not bode well as other business owners will sense this lack of confidence and anxiety. They will potentially believe you aren't confident about your products and services. By changing your thoughts to, 'I can do this', 'everyone in this room is lovely' and 'I am confident about my products and services', you will project a different energy and you will be acting from a positive mindset which will be more effective and will feel better.

In reality, everyone at a network meeting has felt this way at some point in their business career. Most people are scared and anxious when they first start in business and when they go networking and they have no idea how to act. They are out of their comfort zones. Everyone will be empathising with you and want you to do well. No one actually wants you to fail, so it is key for you to pay attention at all times to your thoughts, actions and behaviour.

Remember thoughts can be changed instantly and you want your mindset to be flexible and to not have to see everything in black and white, which is probably caused by you being too stubborn or that you have an academic mind and have to make sense of everything as this is how your mind has been programmed to be. If you have a negative thought, change it instantly and just notice how it changes your mindset about your life, your business and the money you can make.

If you would like to gain new mindset skills such as Reiki, Neuro Linguistic Programming or Mindfulness Meditation, I run workshops on these topics. Please go to www.insightfulminds.co.uk for more information.

Exercise:

How are you really reacting around money?

Hold a £1 coin in the palm of your hand. Have a pen and paper near by.

As you sit quietly feeling the energy of the coin in your hand, take three deep breaths, allow your body to relax, clear your mind from any distractions. When you are ready, answer the first question and write down your response. Note the exact wording of what you are saying in your head. Make sure you don't edit your language to make you feel better. Between each question, clear your mind. Answer from your heart not your head.

How do I feel about money?

How do I look after money?

Exercise (cont.):

What is stopping me from having more money?

How may I have more money?

What else do I need to learn about money?

How important is your health to you?

"To keep the body in good health is a duty...otherwise we shall not be able to keep our mind strong and clear.'
Buddha

YOU MAY FIND THIS an odd question to have in a money mindset book, but in the mind, Health, Wealth and Happiness is interlinked. Your health is your wealth. Often when people are in ill health, they will be worrying about money, even if they have it, which in turn affects their happiness. My clients often have not considered the four aspects of health - spiritual, mental, physical and emotional. We are on a spiritual path in life. Everything that has happened to us, positively and negatively will still be interacting with us in our mind. If we are not living in the present, then we will be triggered back into the past to negative events or into the future due to anxiety.

What is important to you about your health?

Whenever I work with my clients, one of the first exercises I do is to elicit their health values to find out what is really holding them back and to see if they are really looking after themselves. There are always a few surprises. What I have discovered is that most people are blissfully unaware of how they are affected by their thoughts. They just think that life gives them the bad things that have happened e.g. ill health, accidents, negative relationships, etc and are unaware of how by changing their thoughts and the patterns they have in life, they can change their lives for the better. Sometimes there can be patterns of rejection especially if the person has been adopted at birth or an incident in their past has happened where they have experienced rejection such as rejection from a parent or significant other. A person will then look for rejection more in subsequent relationships whether this is within their business or personally.

The reason I like to do this exercise is to give my client a bit of a wake up call and it is a logical process of how in their mind they are negative about their health. Often they are kidding themselves about eating healthily or exercising, but if you don't value yourself, your self worth will be low and it will affect the money that you can earn. The language in your mind linked to your values either motivates you towards what you desire in life or away from it. As you discover in later chapters, your beliefs about money will also be playing a part too.

Having had so many health issues myself, a heart complaint, chronic pain syndrome, high blood pressure, asthma, depression, anxiety, etc, and having recovered naturally, I now have a view that if you have a long term health issue, you are chronically negative in your mind. No one worked on my mindset and thought processes when I was ill and had they, I would not have lost so much time to ill health. Some of my thoughts were conscious but a lot was caused by subconscious thoughts of 'not being good enough' and comparing myself to my very academic and clever twin sister. I now know, you must never compare yourself to another. We are all unique. Actually, I'm really academic and clever too!

Your happiness must always come first in life. Be careful if you are saying to yourself, 'I will be happy when…I get a divorce, a new car, when I go on holiday', as you can chose to be happy right here, right now. It is a choice.

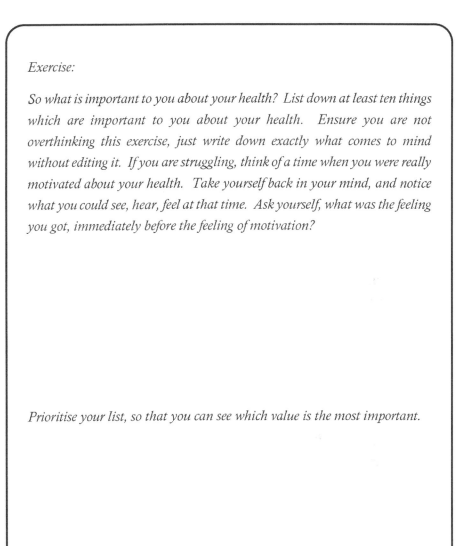

Exercise:

So what is important to you about your health? List down at least ten things which are important to you about your health. Ensure you are not overthinking this exercise, just write down exactly what comes to mind without editing it. If you are struggling, think of a time when you were really motivated about your health. Take yourself back in your mind, and notice what you could see, hear, feel at that time. Ask yourself, what was the feeling you got, immediately before the feeling of motivation?

Prioritise your list, so that you can see which value is the most important.

What values do you need to have the best health?

The exercise above will have identified your values about your health. I deliberately did not tell you what they should be so that you were honest and received the true answer of what you are thinking. They will be your 'conscious' values' rather than what you are believing 'unconsciously'. The key order of health values to have the best all round health is:

- ♥ Happiness
- ♥ Peace of mind (mental health)
- ♥ Healthy eating
- ♥ Exercise
- ♥ Energy

Most people do not have these as their top five and therefore are not motivated enough about their health, even though if they were, they would have more money. Do you have the top five values in the order as listed? No... I'm not surprised. The majority of people don't which is why people get overweight, unhappy and demotivated. Your emotional past will be playing a part unless you have dealt with the emotion and you are now living in the present. This will affect the money you can manifest.

The other health values you may have identified are very individual to the person and what you want to achieve with your health and your life. Obviously, the language in your mind needs to be positive about these values to help you achieve what you are looking for e.g. losing weight, eating healthily, etc. For example someone who has chronic fatigue or ME often says that their top value is to be pain free or to have more energy. Well if the mind is always thinking first that it needs not to be in pain (therefore reminding itself about the pain) or to always need more energy and it never has enough, the body will get very tired, very quickly.

When I work with my clients on a 1-1 basis, we take this exercise much deeper as I analyse the language of their conscious and unconscious mind. This then helps specifically identify what is stopping them from improving their health.

Are you looking after yourself?

Often clients I work with have the belief 'I must work hard' to earn money. Unfortunately, this belief works against them as the harder they work, often the more strain they put on themselves as they are using the wrong strategies for success. The key is actually to be relaxed and work to a plan. You don't necessarily have to 'work hard' to earn money. For example this book is selling while I sleep as it is available on Amazon. In the age of digital technology, things can be really simple but we are still working to outdated beliefs. According to Daniel Priestley in his book, 'Become a Key Person of Influence', 'The harder you work, the less you earn. Your best ideas come out to play, ...not to work'. So true.

Are you covering up how you actually feel by drinking, smoking or taking drugs? Now is the time to face your feelings, to learn how to overcome and change your emotional state and to deal with stress and anxiety in a different way. Using these strategies is just papering over how you really feel and they will affect the success and longevity of your business.

Ask yourself, how much water do I actually drink every day? Most people are not drinking enough and are spending the day dehydrated. If you are dehydrated and thirsty, you will not be able to function properly. Your thought processes and concentration will be affected. We are emotional creatures and all our behaviour is producing negative and positive emotions all the time. We see something on television which makes us feel sad and this adds to the sadness which we may already be carrying such as a bereavement of a family member. We then feel heavier and darker. The processing of our feelings and letting them go, works better if we are hydrated. You are aiming to be as light and bright as possible, so drink more water on a daily basis.

You need to get into a habit of drinking water, every day rather than when you just 'remember'. If you are just 'remembering', you are not prioritising your health which is therefore affecting your wealth! You are looking for yourself to become unconscious competent at drinking water regularly e.g. one glass of water an hour. Just like you don't forget to brush your teeth twice a day, you can do the same with your fluid intake. A new habit has to be completed 28 times in a row. Keep track of your consumption to get the success you desire.

Exercise is also very important and is ignored by so many. It is important that you carry out an exercise that you enjoy rather than something that you think you should do like going to the gym! I love walking my dog Charlie twice a day and this is the main exercise I get, although I do also carry out yoga exercises too and sometimes go swimming. Track how much exercise you actually take. Remember energy is supposed to be moving, so if you are sedate all the time then you are going to be stuck and you will find it more difficult to move forward and change things which you desire including the money you want. Be in flow as much as you can and exercise is a key part of this journey.

Connecting with nature is essential too. Do you live somewhere really urban? If yes, you will need to plan to go to places which are more natural such as the coast, the park or the countryside. When you are within nature, you need to really connect with it. Feel the energy from the plants/trees. Really breathe deeply to take in the air and to connect with yourself. Smell the air and feel it on your skin. Be really mindful and clear your mind of any anxieties when you do this. You will find it easier to meditate in this environment too. Gaining peace by seeing natural things around you will help you live more in the present moment and to appreciate what beauty we have around us if we take long enough to look!

To learn more about valuing health more and to start making positive changes to your thought processes around your health, you may like to come on one of my workshops. Go to www.insightfulminds.co.uk for more information.

3

Beliefs about money - what do you believe?

'What the mind of man can conceive and believe, it can achieve.'
Napoleon Hill

Are your beliefs holding you back?

WHAT YOU BELIEVE ABOUT money and how you can achieve financial success will govern what results you achieve around money in your life. Often we are limiting ourselves by the beliefs we are maintaining that have been programmed into us by the people around us such as our parents, siblings, friends, religious leaders and teachers. We even judge what people will spend based on our own ability to spend money. If we look at something and think something is expensive and we can't afford it, we then project this belief onto another person, but in reality how do you actually know what money a person does or does not have. You don't!

The beliefs we maintain are decisions we make to ourselves when we believe something is true. For example, if you have been told as a child that 'money is always difficult to come by', and you experience this by your parents never having money when you are growing up, you will make a decision to yourself 'money is always difficult to come by', and this is what will happen for you too. You can change this though, by challenging and changing that belief/decision or you may find that someone comes into your life that helps you see a different point of view.

There can be very deeply ingrained spiritual beliefs such as 'it's not ok to charge for my services when healing someone.' I believed this for a long time and gave away thousands of pounds of therapy/coaching to people around me as it just didn't seem right to take money when I was doing something I loved and the people I was helping needed me.

The problem is that my business started to suffer as I just could not sustain this behaviour. I had bills too. Often my clients would say that they had no money, but then they would tell me that they were going on holiday or had paid for something else. The truth was they were not valuing their health or the service I was providing. The only person getting poorer was me!

Often people do not value something that is free as they believe 'it is free, so it will not have any worth or value to it.' The key to valuing something, is appreciating its worth and expressing gratitude for being able to use it/have it. As you give something value and appreciation, you will attract value and appreciation back to you, which will positively impact yourself worth.

We all have conscious and unconscious thoughts and although consciously we may believe one thing, you can actually be sabotaged by your subconscious mind, which is what happened to me. Consciously, I believed that everyone was equal and everyone has the same choices in life and can earn whatever money they wanted. Unconsciously though, I was believing something quite different.

One day, I was visiting a neighbour's house which overlooked the beautiful Weald of Kent. As I looked over the view from their garden towards the Weald, in my head I had a thought 'This is how the other half lives.' Admittedly, the house and grounds are very extensive and would probably be worth in the region of £1 million. When analysing this thought, it is clear that it shows jealousy and envy, which are negative emotions.

Negative emotions repel the money you can earn, so clearly this was not a good thought to have when trying to attract in money. What I should have been thinking is 'lucky neighbours' and been happy for them achieving this level of financial success. They have worked hard for their success. My unconscious thoughts showed that I was judging myself as not as good as my neighbours and that I could not have the same opportunities/money which is just not true.

A very common belief my clients often hold to be true, is that 'life is a battle'. Often they have experienced a tough life so far and therefore their expectation is that life will continue that way. It is important for someone with this belief to change how they are thinking and to remove the resistance towards a life which can be easy and playful. In fact according to the Spirit of Science, 'The less you respond to negativity, the more peaceful your life becomes.', which is so true.

The good news is that you can change your thoughts. It is just a case of paying more attention to the language that you use in your mind - is it positive or negative? If it is negative, you need to start understanding why you are saying these negative things to yourself and change them to be positive. When I learnt about Neuro Linguistic Programming (NLP) it changed my life. I had no idea how negative I was as a person and that by changing how I thought about my life and experiences, I could have a different life. I never really considered that I was creating my life. I just thought things happened which were negative. I learnt to take responsibility for my thinking and what I was creating in my life including the opportunities around money.

If you would like to know more about the Neuro Linguistic Programming training I have on offer for business owners, please visit my website at www.insightfulminds.co.uk.

Exercise:

Close your eyes and clear your mind and imagine walking along a familiar high street to reach your bank. Go inside and approach the bank counter to speak to a bank teller. Ask them if you can access your safe deposit box in the vaults and follow them along a corridor to the lift. As you get in the lift, see that you are already on floor 5 and watch the lift buttons light up from 5-1 as you descend to the basement where the vault is.

Exit the lift and ahead of you are rows and rows of boxes. The bank teller gives you your key and you go forward and then you move to the right hand side to where you know your box is located. You use your key and unlock the box. Open the door to the box and pull out an inner golden box. Transport this box to the table, and open your box.

What is in the box? Is it full of riches such as wads of cash, jewellery, gold bullion, watches, photos of loved ones or is it empty or full of rubbish, costume jewellery and screwed up paper? This is indicative about how your mind is currently appreciating and valuing money. If there is nothing in your box, you may wish to reflect on what would enrich your life and visualise those things coming in to your life.

Negative core beliefs and I am not good enough....

Everyone feels out of balance at some time in their life. We all have ups and downs which we learn from and we get through, one way or another. What you may not realise is that your energy system is pushed out of balance when you are not feeling good and this is based on what you are believing, due to what you have experienced in life. Your thoughts govern everything you do. As you have a thought, you will experience either a positive or negative emotion. This will then govern the action that you take and therefore the results you achieve.

For example, if you have a thought, 'I can't afford that', you will then feel an emotion in your body e.g. guilt and this often leads to more thoughts, and more emotions e.g. I feel so guilty that I can't buy this toy for my daughter's birthday (thought and emotion), you then won't buy the item (action) and this potentially will affect how you interact with your daughter or other people around you (result/behaviour), as you may feel angry or guilty that you can't afford an item.

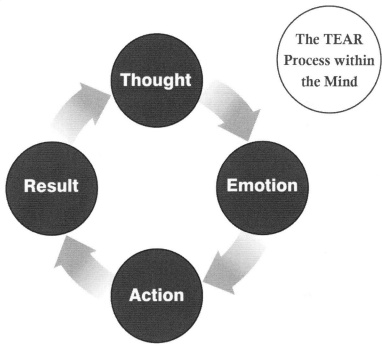

Adapted from 'Stuff for Business' by Ash Lawrence

Are you good enough?

Within the mind, we have core beliefs as to whether we are 'good enough' or 'not good enough'. These are linked to our self worth. There are 11 negative core beliefs which underpin why we don't feel good enough in life, whether that is in relationships, how we are doing at work, friendships, communication, etc.

The key negative core belief that underpins someone's money, generally is around their self worth and they are saying to themselves 'I'm not good enough, I have no value or worth.' As soon as the person works on the emotional issues from the past linked to this belief, they will start to feel better. It is usually because their beliefs about money are false or so deeply ingrained as a negative, that they don't even realise this is affecting their life.

Broad negative core beliefs or feelings about myself:	Life issue related to core beliefs:
1. Not good enough (I am not safe)	Security, safety
2. Not good enough (I don't belong)	Belonging, nurture, self care
3. Not good enough (I have no value, I am worthless)	Self worth
4. Not good enough (I am powerless)	Success, power, control
5. Not good enough (I am wrong, I am unsure)	Reality, reason, knowing
6. Not good enough (My life is out of balance)	Balance, moderation
7. Not good enough (I don't exist; I am nothing)	Identity, recognition
8. Not good enough (I am not real)	Self awareness
9. Not good enough (I am unlovable; unwanted)	Love, loved and loving
10. Not good enough (I am defective)	Health, self healing
11. Not good enough (I am not whole I have lost my spirit)	Wholeness, spirit

Taken from: www.core-beliefs-balance.com/example_negative_core_beliefs.htm

Often we can worry if we are good enough and this can affect our confidence and the results we achieve in life. We can give up too easily on things that we need, as we lack confidence. Perseverance is often needed. Sometimes it is a lesson in life when we find ourselves in a situation where we have to step out of our comfort zone and speak up or ask for something we require. Anxiety which is surrounding a negative core belief needs to be overcome and this is what I help my 1-1 clients overcome easily and effortlessly.

There can also be limiting beliefs which stop us from seeing the richness of life, such as believing that if it rains you can't be happy or have fun. When I have worked with clients with Seasonal Dysfunctional Disorder (SAD syndrome), they always have a belief 'I can't be happy in the winter.' When you ask a person about why they are missing the light so much, they usually have a favourite place that was home previously where they used to enjoy having more light.

For example, they might have lived in the Philippines or Spain, so in their mind, they go back to those 'happy and light' times, but that is living in the past. Light can be brought within by different means through meditation or having a therapy such as Reiki, Emotional Freedom Technique or Time Line Therapy. As you remove the dark, negative and heavy emotions linked to your past, you will instantly feel lighter and brighter. The more you feel good and lighter, the easier you will find it is to manifest the money you desire.

For those business owners who experience a breakup of their marriage or relationships whilst in business, this can be because their partner does not believe in them or what they are doing because of their own insecurities or 'stuff from the past'. Any business owner will start to feel not good enough if their partner is not on board as you need a joint vision and this can cause more anxiety and depression. It is so much easier if your partner is there to support you. If you are in a situation of being on your own, then believe in yourself, always chase your dreams, and surround yourself with those who

Exercise:

Money is…..Discover your money beliefs

Write down the words Money is…. and finish the statement. Money is……powerful. Money is…… dirty. Money is ….hard to come by, etc. Create ten or more statements about your beliefs about money. Just let your thoughts flow. Now look at what you have written and decide if it is a positive, negative or neutral statement to have made. Often you will uncover some very unusual beliefs about money and often they really are not positive at all. Anything negative which comes up, you will need to reframe into a positive in future. If you have Money is… security. This is not a good thing. This shows that you are not trusting the Universe to bring you money and shows that the emotion of insecurity is too high in your body.

believe in you and you will succeed. Get yourself a buddy and work as a team to motivate one another.

My lack of maths ability, linked to an emotional event from the past, meant that every time I focussed on anything related to numbers, I developed a strategy where I felt anxiety. This is a habit I had created based on my thoughts. I had a belief, 'I must get anxious when I see numbers'. I am now aware of this problem and have 'healed' the emotional issue from the past which made me feel inadequate around numbers. In my business, I have taken time to learn more about money management and financial planning. I still do not love doing anything around numbers (it's just not my thing) but I now understand what needs to happen in my business to make it successful and profitable. I know this is an area for me to gain expert advice and I have brilliant experts helping and guiding me.

Recently I asked myself why I was still resisting in learning more about numbers and why I found it such a strain and in my head, the thought was 'it's not fair.' When I asked myself, 'what was not fair?' I uncovered another belief 'maths is not fun!' When I reflected back to my past, I realised that it was not fair that my twin sister had Mr Mars who was a fun maths teacher at primary school and I had Mrs Minehead, who was very strict and not much fun at all! When you start paying attention to what you are saying to yourself, you will uncover all sorts of stuff that is holding you back from being the best you can be. It is now time for you to become much more self aware!

Each person's money issues are personal and will relate to their spiritual path. If you would like to understand your beliefs more then you may like to book for a complimentary discovery session with me. www.insightfulminds.co.uk Create what you desire in life. Set your goals and work towards what you want to achieve.

Exercise:

What do you think might be blocking you from having the money you desire?

Exercise:

List 5 simple actions you can take to unblock your flow of money.

4

Law of attraction and money

'I am convinced that there are universal currents of Divine Thought vibrating the ether everywhere and that any who can feel the vibrations is inspired.'
Richard Wagner

THE INSPIRATIONAL FILM AND book 'The Secret' by Rhonda Byrne were created in 2006. Within them, she explored the natural universal law of the Law of Attraction. The basic concepts were that we create our own lives from our thoughts and interactions and by using positive thoughts and behaviours, we can 'attract' what we want into our lives. For example, if you give love to someone, you will receive it back. If you give money to someone, you will get it back (not necessarily from the same person though!)

The key steps to getting the Law of Attraction to work are 'Ask', 'Believe' and 'Receive' and you have to take inspired action to receive what you had asked for. To get the law to work fully, you have to be very specific about what you want, visualise it and feel grateful for what you asked for as if you already have it. By taking inspired action, you are putting energy towards the goal you have asked for and you then have to not question how the outcome will arrive. You also have to fully trust the process and that the Universe will provide for you. This is why it is key to get your beliefs in check!

So who do you ask? What does 'Ask The Universe?' actually mean?

'Ask the Universe for what you want' is used so much, but do you really understand what it means? Are you asking for what you want and nothing is happening?

You create your own universe from your thoughts, feelings, beliefs and attitude. When you think positively, set goals and take action to achieve them, you will attract in people, experiences and events which enable you to achieve your goals and to have the life you desire. You also have to have an attitude of gratitude. Everything comes from your energy field - your universe. It sounds simplistic, but when you start paying attention to your thoughts, beliefs and actions, you will notice more about how life is playing out for you positively and negatively.

As Dr Wayne Dyer said in his film 'The Shift', 'You attract what you are not what you want.' For example, if you want more love in your life, you need to give more love, if you want more money, you need to give money, if you want more freedom, you need to allow yourself to be free. Get the idea!

Depending on your circumstances, your income will change depending on your thought patterns, beliefs and attitude around money. If for example you suddenly lose a regular client or contract, and you continue spending in the same way as when you had them, you could start getting yourself into debt. This is because you have not changed your thoughts and spending habits.

The spiritual attitude to work from is about being grateful for the money you have, are going to have and enjoying the richness of life around us, not just focusing on what bills you have to pay. If you are worrying about having a lack of money (negative thoughts), you are pushing away the very thing that you are trying to attract. Everything is attracted in via your thought patterns.

___

You have to work on keeping yourself in alignment with the Law of Attraction. It is really important to look after your health to attract in the wealth you desire. You have to be feeling good and have high energy to get the law to work quickly for you. You can literally manifest in seconds if you want to!

If you haven't read 'The Secret' and 'The Magic' by Rhonda Byrne, I suggest that you do. You will feel inspired and will see a completely different view of life and your application of money. It is essential that you maintain a positive attitude and feel positive emotions. This helps you manifest what you want to attract into your life and business. You also need to be looking how you can serve others by helping them, which helps you detract from the ego. Money will flow to you more easily.

The basics of 'Ask the Universe' is to ask for what you desire in your thoughts and set SMART goals around this. Ask within your meditations for what you desire and actually take action to ask people around you to help you or overcome something which has previously been a problem by taking inspired action to change things. When you 'Ask' for what you want, the next steps are to 'Believe' you deserve to receive it and then 'Receive' it into your life.

Focus on what you desire with passion and excitement. It is essential to visualise what you want when you are in a happy state and when you feel good. Feel grateful for what you have in life now and for what you would like to receive. If you have asked for something that you just don't believe will happen, then it won't work.

For example, you say to yourself, I want to earn £1m by the end of the year. Your subconscious mind will not agree that this is possible as it does not have any evidence from the past to agree you can be this successful. Start small and get bigger with the financial goals that you set.

Reasons for the Universe not providing you what you want....

- ♥ This is because you do not believe that what you are asking for is possible e.g. to earn £100,000 in 3 months

- ♥ You are not open to receiving help, support, money into your life e.g. you feel embarrassed when someone wants to help you or give you money

- ♥ You aren't taking enough inspired action to achieve the goals that you have set

- ♥ You are being too negative. You need to work more on changing your emotions to be positive. Live with love, joy, happiness, excitement, passion, and fun rather than anger, fear, stubbornness, guilt, powerlessness, hopelessness, fear, anxiety, and distrust

- ♥ You need to change your thoughts from being scarcity based to being abundant. Prosperity comes in many forms - money, new ideas, discounts, friendship, nature, meals paid for by friends which means you don't have to cook. The list is endless

- ♥ You haven't planned enough for what you are hoping to receive. Plan all the steps to getting the money you would like to receive. For example, if you are putting on an event - What resources do you need? Who can help you? What venue will you use? Act as if something is happening, not that it 'might' happen

- ♥ You are living from your ego, not the true you. Always look at how you can serve others

- ♥ You are not grateful enough for what you do have. Say to yourself, 'I'm so happy and grateful that I now have....' Appreciate what you have at the moment. State what you desire. Believe that something is already yours. Unwavering faith. You don't need to know how the universe will bring what you want, just trust that it will come to you and take inspired action!! Go for it......have the life you want to have

♥ You are being too rigid in your thinking. Be careful of black and white thoughts. These thoughts are not flexible enough. Remember thoughts are energy and energy is supposed to be moving not stuck!! Are you a stubborn person? If so, change your thinking to be more flexible. Change is good and allows you to go with the flow

The personal qualities of being attractive to the Universe

To be fully attractive to the Universe and to get the Law of Attraction to work best, there are specific personal qualities that you need to possess to heighten your personal attractiveness. The chart over the page helps indicate what these are. If you find some of your qualities are on the unattractive side, then start changing your thoughts, behaviour and your actions. If necessary, get some therapy to help you become more positive! Remember 'You attract what you are, not what you want'. Dr. Wayne Dyer.

If you are thinking, 'I'm really quite unattractive' at the moment, then now is the time to move yourself from being unattractive to attractive. The journey of becoming attractive can be really fun or it can feel like hard work. This is because you have conscious and unconscious behaviour which needs to change. You can make small and simple changes on a regular basis and this will make a difference. I love working with my clients to help them move from 'unattractive' to 'attractive' and to make that journey much, much easier. Often you can't spot what the changes are that you need to make and this is where I give my clients a unique insight based on my wisdom and experience.

The analysis of the spiritual path I carry out before I meet a client, means that I can precisely target the negative core beliefs they have of 'not feeling

Attractive	Unattractive
Abundance	Scarcity
Living in the present	Stuck in the past
Joy with life	Lack of joy from life
Happy	Depressed
Enlightened and empowered	Disempowered
Have self belief/faith	Lack of self belief/faith
Not anxious (knowing the future)	Anxious (fearing the future)
Ease/relaxed	Dis-ease/stressed
Learning life lessons	Not learning the lessons - repeating patterns
Feeling loved	Feeling unloved
Positive	Negative
Non judgemental	Being judgemental of self and others
Feeling gratitude deeply	Taking people and things for granted
Listening to others	Telling others what to do!
Energised	Lacking energy/tired
Giving and receiving easily	Receiving and not giving
Forgiving self and others	Unforgiving - not forgiving self and others
Generous (with time, money and friendship)	Mean (with time, money and friendship)
Feeling light and bright	Feeling dark and heavy
Honest with self and others	Telling lies to self and others
Helping others (selfless)	Considering only yourself and not others
Having fun and laughing lots	Misery. Isolating yourself and not doing what you want to do.
Feeling connected with self and others	Feeling disconnected, isolated and lonely
Unstuck and motivated	Stuck and demotivated

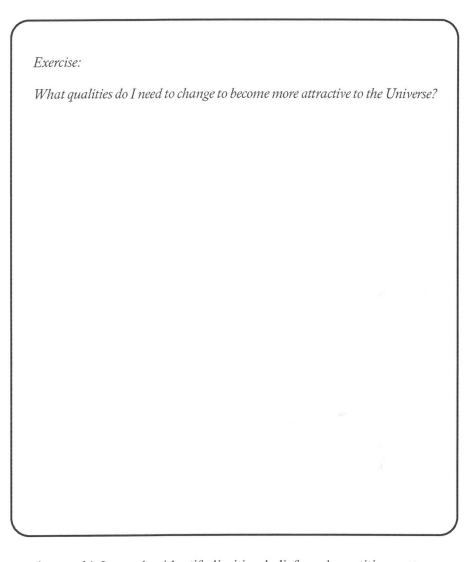

Exercise:

What qualities do I need to change to become more attractive to the Universe?

good enough'. I can also identify limiting beliefs and repetitive patterns as well as mentoring them about what they need to change about themselves to make life so much better and to make the money that they desire in their business. If you would like to know more about 1-1 coaching sessions or workshops, go to www.insightfulminds.co.uk.

Working on yourself first, carrying out personal development before investing in other things, will give you a faster route to earning the money you desire to enable you to have the life you desire. If you have a business, then it is essential to understand yourself first and what you want to achieve in life, before you invest in other aspects of your business such as your website, graphic design, advertising, video, promotion etc.

Achieve peace of mind

When you are in tune with yourself, you also need to display other qualities as well which help you through the challenges of being a business owner.

Peace stands for:

P   Perseverance

E   Emotional Health

A   Attitude

C   Control

E   Evolving

Perseverance

To have true success in your business, you have to perseverance. There are many challenges and 'curve balls' in business and you have to become resilient to ride the waves and to keep going. The mantra 'Never Give Up' has always served me well and my determination to succeed. Even if you are having a bad day and your self belief is wavering, start focusing on the positives and the hidden blessings in disguise. Remember bad moments pass. It is how you are reacting to them. If things are feeling so difficult, ask yourself why? Are you putting yourself under too much pressure or worried about how others are judging you? You have to stand in your power and have unwavering faith.

Persistence is also key. Often people give up too soon in business due to fear of rejection. Sometimes you have to try things many times to be heard about your idea or to get through to the right person who can help you. Be persistent. If you know your product or service is excellent and you need others to know it, be bold, have self belief and try all avenues with the attitude of 'I will never give up' to be heard and to be seen.

Emotional Health

Business is a rollercoaster of emotions, going up and down the scale from depression and fear right up to love, joy, happiness, appreciation and freedom. Your job is to pay attention to emotions in your body by sensing them within you as you feel them and to work on how to shift the negative ones from your body, so that you only work from a positive vibration. This can be achieved by a variety of techniques such as Timeline Therapy, Reiki, Hypnosis, Emotional Freedom Technique, and Meditation. Some techniques you can learn yourself and others you need to see a practitioner like myself.

Drink at least two litres of water a day to keep hydrated as you are processing emotions every day which is tiring and the body is made up of 80% water, so needs to be re-hydrated, especially if you have been in a negative or stressful environment. The negative emotions you are feeling are linked to your past or the future, and you need to release them to allow yourself to live in the present moment. The lighter and brighter you feel and the more joyous, the easier it is to manifest your dreams and money!!

Attitude

An attitude of Gratitude is an absolute must for gaining peace of mind and to build up appreciation for your life. We live life so fast and miss many of the details of life which bring us happiness, laughter and fun. Being appreciative and grateful to others, will build up your relationships and you will have a happier life. Make sure you say thank you to those around you especially when you have received help or referrals. The other person may become resentful if you don't thank them and they can cut off sending you any work as you did not show appreciation.

You also need to live with an attitude of Success. Believing in yourself and knowing you are successful is a must. If you ever find yourself saying 'When I am successful!' to others or yourself, you need to assess why, as you are missing daily successes which all feed into the big wins. Often we can view success as when we achieve financial gain, but there are many other things in life apart from money which show us that we are successful. An attitude of Positivity is essential too. Your positivity will rub off on others and everyone has a better day when they are positive. Remember that HOPE stands for Have Only Positive Expectations. You get what you expect, so make sure you expect positive things to happen.

Control

Letting go of control within your business can be one of the hardest things to do. As everything comes from what you think about, it can be easy to think that you have to do everything yourself. When you have the funds to do so, you must outsource jobs which you don't love or get staff to cover those roles. If you don't delegate properly to staff, then they will leave as they won't feel valued and trusted. No one wants to be micro managed. Your need to control is linked to anxiety and distrust issues and will derail your business if you don't learn how to release control and to trust that people around you, will support you.

Trusting and 'letting go' is also about trusting the process and flow of life. Relaxing and allowing the Universe to provide you with everything rather than you stressing that your life is not going the way you had wanted. It is also important to note that others do not control you, although you may think that they do. You are in full control about how you react to others and the results you get from this communication. You get what you expect.

Letting go and trusting the Universe to provide for you financially and to enable you to fulfil your dreams takes absolute belief and faith. When you trust your inner guidance system, you can literally ask yourself which meetings to go to, who to work with, what you need to do next in your business and just trust the guidance you are given. It is magical when you fully let go of all anxiety and just 'know' what is right or wrong for you. When you trust your own wisdom, you will be guided to places, people and external guidance you need to build your business. Some people say, they are 'magnetised' to me. This is just their internal guidance system directing them. When we start chatting, it is always clear why we are in each other's lives.

Evolving

We are all 'work in progress' and evolving. Sometimes we are going through life too quickly, so we are sent life lessons to learn, such as learning to slow down, to appreciate our health and to be grateful for what we have in our life. Mindfulness meditation is a fantastic way to learn how to slow down, refocus and to get in tune with ourselves.

As we put at the forefront of our minds, what we want to achieve in our lives and who we want to be so that we are fulfilled, we evolve into the people we are meant to be which gives us peace of mind. No one wants to have regrets, so always focus on evolving into the person you want to be. In business it is essential that you are authentic. You need to be the same person at home as you are within your business rather than putting on a persona as this is what you think people want to see. People buy from people and they will see right through you if you are not walking your talk. Practice what you preach and dress how you want to, not how you 'think' you should dress.

Your personal branding all depends on who you are and what your business is about. You may be spending money on promotional activities which will yield you no work as it is not aimed at your niche or even the type of work you are meant to be focussing on. I made poor investments in my website design and getting promotional material created that in the end I could not use as my path changed from being an educational consultant to what I was meant to be doing which was being a healer, therapist, coach and mentor. Looking back, it probably cost me at least £1000.

5

Taking responsibility

'Live as if you were to die tomorrow. Learn as if you were to live forever.'
Mahatma Gandhi

TAKING RESPONSIBILITY FOR ALL (and I mean all) your actions takes guts. It is so easy to blame someone else for something that has happened in your life and for the mess you are in financially. If you are not making the money that you want to make, you are not taking full responsibility. If you are in debt, taking responsibility for sorting out your 'money mess' can be hard, especially if you have been living life like an ostrich, but when you finally take control and open all those bills you have been ignoring, make the phone calls to your creditors and add up what you owe, your life will change. I know, because I have had to do it.

Painful as it was to phone the Stepchange debt charity for help and guidance. I did it and it was such a relief when I had. Thankfully they are incredibly non-judgemental and really helpful. Interestingly, the day that I rang them and took full responsibility, I had a call out of the blue offering me work worth £500! So.....what are you ignoring?

The more I take responsibility for understanding and knowing exactly what money I have and which bills I have to pay, the more in control I am and my money grows. When I ignore it, as it feels easier that way sometimes, opportunities to make money diminish. The key is learning to understand money, the terminology around money as well as changing the strategies and beliefs you have around money, especially if you are finding it hard to do this. When you don't know how to understand money, then ask for help. There are lots of people around you who want to help you, but often you need to ask them to give them permission to help you.

Get yourself a bookkeeper or accountant and get them to teach you what things mean financially in your business. Be careful not to abdicate all responsibility to them though, as you need to track your money and know what you can and can't spend. Work in a partnership with one who you can trust and communicate easily with.

Are you acting like a victim or blaming others or yourself?

There are two ways in life. Living your life with brilliance and making positive choices or acting as the victim and making excuses. In Neuro Linguistic Programming (NLP), it is called living your life from Cause or Effect. By learning from what is going on and making positive choices about taking responsibility, life will change for the better. This is living your life at Cause.

In your mind, you may fall back into Effect, where your mind is saying 'but it is their fault', 'I've failed', 'I can't do it, it feels too hard' or 'I'm not good enough or worthy'. You have to take control of those thoughts. You have a choice. Think positive thoughts and keep moving yourself over towards living your life at Cause.

Another way of looking at this, is to see whether you are learning from what is going on in your life or are you blaming yourself or others? Taking responsibility takes courage, but when you intend to make a change, you will find that things will start to happen to make it easier for you to do so. If you would like know more about how to change your behaviour then you might like to work with me on a 1-1 basis or attend a course on Neuro Linguistic Programming. Go to www.insightfulminds.co.uk for more details.

Exercise:

What is your biggest fear about money?

Look into a mirror and say to yourself 'my biggest fear about money is....'
Pay attention to the feelings and fears that come up. Write them down and
look at what you are saying to yourself. You can then start taking action.

Are you trying to do it all by yourself?

When you are depressed or feeling down, you naturally isolate yourself. You don't love yourself, so why would anyone want to love you. The more you do this, the more you start to think, no one will help you. You start to feel bad and your vibe goes down. Loneliness is a sign that you need to pay attention to as well, as it can really affect you. I hadn't appreciated just how lonely I would be when I started my own business. I had not appreciated that I was a member of four different teams when I was employed and then when I started my business it was just me.

Actually, there are always people in life who want to help you and you have to let them. Sometimes you have been such a giver yourself for so long, that you have forgotten that there needs to be a natural flow of receiving too and this may well be one of your lessons in life. Being a receiver is essential to getting the flow of money right in your life. Allow your friends, family and networking colleagues support and help you, and notice how much easier it is to do business.

The easiest way to move forward in your business is to have joint ventures and collaborating. Ensure you help others and they will then help you. What goes around comes around. If you are not receiving love from those around you, you are probably not loving yourself enough. According to Daniel Priestley, Richard Branson has 150 Joint Ventures with other businesses within the Virgin group. So who can you get to help you and to empower you to earn the money you desire to have the lifestyle you want? For more information about being a better receiver see Chapter 7 about learning lessons in life.

Asking for help takes guts, but when you start asking others to help you, you will find so much love and support around you, this will inspire you to make the changes you need to make. You will feel empowered. Spiritually, other people have to give and you asking them empowers them to get the flow of energy working right for them too. If you know how to meditate, ask yourself before going into your meditation, who could help you and see who pops up in your head when your meditation ends.

This is a lesson in life that I had to learn. I was trying to sort my dire financial situation out on my own and wasn't making much headway. I've had to ask for help when I just couldn't physically find any money to pay for things. I was so stressed and down that the techniques I share in this book couldn't work. I had help from family, friends and networking buddies, and I am so grateful to them. I also had to get used to asking for simple things, which would save me money.

There was a builder next door and I asked him one day if I could have the wood he was throwing away for my wood burner and also cheekily I asked if he would chop it up into small pieces for me. He replied 'If you don't ask, you don't get!' (what a great lesson!) and every day until he finished his job, a small pile of chopped wood appeared on my patio from him. Such a lovely man and I really appreciated being kept warm over the winter for free!

This lesson deepens too if you are not allowing your partner, husband or wife to help you sort out the finances whether you are in debt or not. If you are taking too much responsibility for it as I was, this is a real problem. It is essential that as a couple, you share responsibility of looking at the finances together and ensuring that you don't get into debt or plan together how you are going to sort out the financial trouble together. A joint vision for the life you desire together is essential. By only one person taking responsibility, the other partner will feel naturally more insecure.

This is a really common problem I help my clients with. My own need to keep control of the finances and to try to sort it out myself, affected my husband's self worth, as a man's underlying desire in life is to be able to provide for a woman. If you have no idea about your joint finances, take responsibility now and change this. Speak to your partner and get involved. If you struggle with numbers as I did, then let your partner track things, but get involved and let them teach you how they do it. If you are both bad with numbers, get external help! There is a lot out there for free to help you if you look or ask someone for help!

Change your habits

Now is the time to change your habits. Some of our habits just don't work for us and you need to identify which money habits are just not working for you. One thing I did was track all the things that I tell my clients to do to gain financial success over a 28 day period. I was then able to see what I was consistent with and more importantly what I wasn't doing. My tracker then gave me the evidence I needed to be able to make changes to my routine. To help you, you can download the money habit tracker template from www.insightfulminds.co.uk.

As you will see from the tracker, it is not just traditional money habits that you need to start changing. As your health is your wealth, you need to start changing your habits around your health to make the biggest impact as well as improving on your money management habits. For example, when you wake up, do you meditate? Do you visualise the day ahead and feel gratitude for the day ahead being amazing? Probably not, so these are habits to get into. When you start to take more control about what you are thinking and changing the bad habits you are in, you will start to notice the transformation in your life and your finances will become more healthy too.

When you are in debt, there can be real fear about how to sort it out. The more anxious you become about sorting it out, the more you are making the situation worse. Taking action to sort out debt takes courage as well as looking at your debt and being honest. Work out a plan of how to pay back the money. Create a strategy to repay the money. Your strategy of worrying or being an ostrich about your finances is not working and makes you feel much worse.

If you are not earning as much as you would like, you might be in the habit of only earning money in a particular way. For example, you may be a health food shop. You are lacking in customers and your custom in the shop may be diminishing. It might be that you need an internet presence or to start sending out a newsletter to your customers and suppliers. Send them discounts, promotions and useful information like events and recipes. Your habit of never using technology, could be really affecting your financial ability.

Another habit which affects a person's finances is the ability to speak up. If you are the sort of person who always does something for free, ask yourself why you are in this habit pattern. For what reason are you not valuing yourself? It is time to practise saying no or asking for money for your time/service rather than just giving it away. Once you have done it a few times, you will find that actually your client often wants to pay for your service and feels embarrassed not paying.

Speak up and talk to your partner if you find it difficult not understanding the finances and this makes you feel insecure. Working on your finances together is essential for a happy and romantic partnership. Often there can be a belief 'I can't speak up.' which is lurking and suppressing what you can achieve. In business, you have to be visible and speak up about your brand. Are you doing this or are you hiding, pretending that you are doing it but not putting a lot of effort into it?

Other habits you might like to consider changing are not spending everything in your purse. You should be saving at least 10% of your income. You need to be able to show the Universe that you respect money and that you don't need to spend it all. Most people spend all the money they have and more (i.e. on credit). Appreciate what you do have, without going into debt. Play at being frugal. Ask for discounts and to make savings where you can. Ask yourself 'Do I want this or need this?' Only buy things that you need and save up for things that you want. You will feel more in control of your money.

It is a fact that the majority of lottery winners have spent their money within five years as they have not adopted the correct money behaviours and habits to keep the money flowing. You don't have to win the lottery to be rich though, as you can be rich in so many ways such as being in love, appreciating friends, being helped by those around you or just appreciating the beauty of nature.

Be careful not to transfer behaviour too e.g. if you can't buy clothes from shops due to shortage of money, so you buy them from the charity shop instead. Basically you are buying clothes to make yourself feel better rather than dealing with the deeper emotional issues going on inside you. If you are in a habit of avoiding looking at your bank account regularly, then get into a habit of looking at it and being ok with it not showing a healthy balance yet. Get into a habit of visualising your bank account with money in it.

Are you in a habit of feeling bad about not being able to pay your bills? One habit I changed, was to ensure all my bills came to me as paper bills rather than on direct debit. I write on every bill which arrives, 'thank you for the money' and trust that the money will come to pay it. When I pay the bill, I write on the bill, 'thank you paid' and feel gratitude for being able to pay it. With the digital age, we have so many things to pay electronically, it is often easy to pay for something and not value and appreciate the fact that you have the money to be able to pay for it. Ensure that you also feel gratitude as you are invoicing your clients too, as it is a blessing that they are paying on time and for your services.

Are you in a habit of mediating everyday? If not, this is an essential one to start as this will relax you and give you more focus and appreciation of your day. Taking time for you is essential. Also set goals every day linked to your personal vision, so that you are directing your thoughts towards what you would love in your life, rather than what you don't want. The money will be found quicker when you plan how to bring what you would like into your life.

Do you know how much money you currently have and are you clear about how much you want? Think of money as a new friend or date. The more you take ownership of your money management, the more you can define what money you would like to see in your life. Are you good at maths? If not, learn how to feel good around numbers. Get into a habit of doing something 'numbers' related every day. Do free online tests to get better at it or ask a friend to teach you how to manage your money effectively and as you get out of debt, to be able to save and invest effectively.

If you notice that you have extreme avoidance in sorting out the numbers, then this is linked to your self worth. If you can't sort out your behaviour and it is too much of a struggle, then I would be happy to help you via my workshops and 1-1 coaching/therapy. For more information, go to www.insightfulminds.co.uk.

Some important habits to create if you are not abundant in money yet, is to allow the money to flow. Money is energy and it is supposed to be moving. You need to be able to give money freely and receive it. If you don't easily give it away by being generous (you should give 10% away), then ask yourself what is the fear about giving the money away? It may bring up insecurity feelings that need to be dealt with. It is important to only give away money when you are out of debt yourself though. I have worked with clients who are giving so much away to charity now because they think the charities are in need and feel emotionally drawn to do so and have not planned for their financial futures and retirement. This is an ineffective strategy which will just cause you more long term stress.

Another habit to embed is to save 10% of your money. You may say, 'I just can't do that. I never have any money to spare.' You would be surprised about what you can save when you try. Shopping in a lower priced supermarket for example could save you that 10%. You may have clutter all around your house that you could sell on Ebay. Look at how much food you waste each week and ensure that it isn't wasted.

Exercise:

Where am I giving up responsibility about money in my life? E.g. not ringing Stepchange, ringing your creditors rather than hiding or being an ostrich around your finances?

If you had all the money you desire - how would you spend it? Compile a list of what you would like to do. How would you live your life differently? How would money empower you? How would you being rich benefit the world? Would your money disappear as quickly as it arrived?

Many of my clients are not spending any of the money that they earn on themselves. Often all money goes on their kids or someone else. To value yourself, you need to start to get into a habit of spending 10% of your income on yourself. This might be buying yourself a new dress once in a while, having your nails done or going on a day trip somewhere. The important thing is that you are rewarding yourself for your hard work and are looking after yourself.

If you are in debt, be responsible and create a plan to pay off the debt but also have fun too. Stepchange charity will help you do this if things are really feeling too much for you. Concentrate on paying off your debts first before you start saving and giving to charity.

This will take a weight off you emotionally and allow you to feel more in control. Ensure that you do give yourself mini treats as rewards for being able to pay off the debt (otherwise you will feel in permanent denial of any pleasure) but just look at how you can reward yourself more cheaply. For example you could go to your local college and get the beauty students to give you a facial or a manicure as this would save you money or a friend may lend you a book that you want to read rather than you buying it.

6

Valuing yourself

'Your worth consists in what you are and not in what you have.'
Thomas Edison

How well do you value yourself?

A S YOU HAVE DISCOVERED from Chapter 3, your beliefs about money can really affect how you value yourself and how you come across in life. Your self worth is intrinsically linked to your past and whether you feel 'good enough or not.' When you get to the point of feeling great and good enough, you are then in alignment with how life is meant to be - relaxed and happy. You will then find it much easier to manifest money as you will know how to plan in your business to achieve success. If you have the incorrect money beliefs, you will be limiting your ability to make money even if you value yourself though, so ensure that these are corrected and you have changed all your bad money habits!

When you are not feeling good enough and not valuing yourself, you are pushing away the very success which you are craving. Unconsciously you can be giving off negative thoughts about being good enough. For example, you may be waiting for your new client to turn up. You start wondering will they show up? Will they like you? Will they think that your prices are too high? and then you get the text or call, telling you that they aren't coming or they just don't show up.

I used to really under value myself and my services. I could manifest within seconds of a negative thought, a text saying my new client wasn't coming. I've had to learn to value the skills, experience and value I have acquired (I have spent at least £40000 on my personal development) and to keep my thoughts positive! If I notice myself wondering if a person will show up, I reframe my thoughts and trust that the person is just delayed and is on their way. I also ensure that my clients now pay me in advance of coaching or attending workshops, so that they are valuing what they receive too. Generally people do not value things which they receive for free, but when they invest their money in something, they give it more value.

I used to find with the events I put on, that people booked late. They were often holding out for a better offer such as a client they may have, rather than booking with the intention of taking on board the information they were taught. This showed that they were living from scarcity. It is so common to see this behaviour at network events too. Network hosts often give up their time for free and this generosity can be abused by the people who attend the events. They don't book in until the last minute or say they are coming and then don't turn up with no notice given. The host may be paying for a venue and with minimum numbers this may affect the viability of a group running and it can also be embarrassing if no one shows up!! The confidence of the host or trainer running the event can be dented!

If you go to networks, it is important to value the host and to attend regularly. Book in advance and if something really does come up which is totally unavoidable, then cancel. Never say you are going to attend an event unless you are really going to. The organiser may be using the information you have given them to justify whether to go ahead or cancel an event. I know I have lost money on booking a venue before.

In Neuro Linguistic Programming, one of the frames which make up how we interact as humans is 'Perception is Projection.' If you are not valuing your health, experience and services, then you will attract other people into your life who don't value you in this way. It is really important to be emotionally stable and to find your value and worth in business. Otherwise, you will start to resent the people around you who are using your services. You may give them hours extra of your time because you are trying to please them, but they just keep asking for more time and you keep giving it and not charging for the extra time/resources.

When you are new in business, often you will give something for free, to allow your networking colleagues to try out your services. This is a great thing to do initially, but as people know what you do, be careful about giving away too much. You may limit it to a free 30 minute or one hour trial. You have worked hard to gain the qualifications, skills and experience that you have and now is the time to value them.

As you value yourself, you will find it easier to charge higher prices as you will be in demand if you are excellent at what you do. Often there are hidden costs in business and you will be completing additional work when you are not in front of your clients/customers. Ensure that your customers know what they are paying for and that you let them know exactly what is included in the service that they get. Remember if you charge a price, people value it more. You can always take a deposit and refund it to them later if you wish.

For example, when I run my complimentary discovery sessions, I ensure that my potential clients know that although the first session is three hours long, that actually they are getting five hours of my time as I will have analysed their life history and written up notes to aid our session and to make it as focussed as possible. I am providing added value. I am also ensuring that they don't waste time in the three hours together on filling in a consent form as I send this ahead to my clients, so that they can fill it in and read the terms and conditions at their leisure.

Before the session, I am planning what is the fastest way I can get a great result for my client as I only want to work with them for the time that they need rather than setting up a dependency model. I want to empower them and send them on their way, so that I can then help more business owners. This allows me to serve more people.

According to 'The Go Giver' by Bob Burg and John David Mann, the amount of money you have is a reflection of the amount of value you have for yourself and how well you are serving your community with your services and product. 'The Law of Value - Your true worth is determined by how much more you give in value than you take in payment.' and 'The Law of Compensation - Your income is determined by how many people you serve and how well you serve them.'

If you are not valuing yourself and your services, how will you communicate the value to your customers. By building up an excellent reputation and offering great customer service, you will serve more people. By valuing your business by investing in great systems and processes for your business you will be able to serve more people effectively and efficiently which will lead to greater income. Of course, if you don't charge enough from the beginning, you will go out of business as you aren't covering your own personal and business expenses and therefore making a profit. Again, if figures are not your thing, ask for help.

It is really important to look at the bigger picture. By valuing yourself, you are helping others. If you don't feel good enough, you aren't giving out the right message or energy to your customers and they will potentially not feel valued enough too. Keeping in touch with your customers by ringing them or sending out a newsletter and valuing their opinions and feedback will help you keep your existing customer base. Mapping out your customer journey will allow you to see if you are valuing your customers and serving them well enough.

There are other ways of valuing yourself which you may not have considered too. How much time are you taking away from your business for you? How many holidays are you taking? Are you regularly taking days off or are you working every day manically trying to get everything done? Are you so focused on your business, that relationships around you such as your partner, friends and family are being affected negatively as you aren't giving them any time?

The key to valuing yourself is getting the work/life balance correct and often with a small business owner looking after your health can take a back seat especially if you are living from a scarcity mindset. I can't stress enough, systems and processes in your business will allow you to take the time out and to manage your finances so that you can take a holiday.

It is really important to consider what your life values are and then to look at your health, finance, relationship and work values. Are they well balanced? Does your life really reflect how you want it to be? This is the time to be really honest with yourself.

Are you spending enough time properly relaxing?

Have you ever considered that maybe you are doing too much? You are giving so much to others and not having time for yourself. You start to feel guilty because you can't have time for yourself? Or you might think, 'I have to keep going to get this work done' to be able to get the money I need. It is an incorrect belief to believe that 'the more you do, the more you are worth.' You may also find yourself overwhelmed by the amount of information that is bombarding you every day via email, Messenger, Facebook, Twitter, etc. The 'noise' from different sources can be deafening!

Bizarrely enough, taking time out for a day off or even a week if you can and not doing 'stuff' will relax you and help reenergise you. It is a mistake to think, 'I must keep busy' or 'I must not relax' - both are beliefs which you might be holding as true. You may be finding that you are living in the 'doing' mode of life and not just 'being'. When you are in the 'doing' mode, you are multi tasking, adding more to your things to do list and not getting it done, which you find frustrating. It is so tiring living in this mode and it will affect your energy levels.

By just 'being' and spending time relaxing, you will actually achieve more tasks, feel more focussed and your concentration is better. Being mindful of how you are reacting in different situations is useful as well as carrying out regular meditation. Taking a walk in a woods or by the seaside can clear the mind and reenergise you to be more effective when you get back to work.

You also will find that you are not using effective strategies to work efficiently and effectively. When you plan more and ensure that you take regular breaks, you will get more done. Taking the regular breaks is an essential step towards valuing yourself and looking after your health. Remember, your health is your wealth! If you find yourself not being able to take holidays or days off as there are always things to do, then you are not relaxing properly and this will affect your energy and the quality of your work. You will put unnecessary pressure on yourself to earn money and in time, you will lose days off work due to colds, viruses or something more chronic!

Taking regular time to meditate every day will make a difference. Learn to delegate tasks which don't interest you or which take you a lot of time. From a work perspective, it is better to spend 90 minutes fully focused with no distractions, and then have a break for 20 minutes rather than working solidly for three hours. Remember your body is energy and is supposed to move!!

If you need to become more convinced about valuing your time, then workout how many hours you have left to live, if you lived to the average age of 80 years old. This will re-focus you to never waste time again. Time is precious. Be careful not to take time for granted and to do things that you love doing. Don't procrastinate about what to do. Do it anyway. If you are not happy about your situation, then do something about it. The quality of your life is how you spend your time. Be careful that you spend your time doing activities that you love and enjoy.

What is stopping you from valuing yourself?

Are you finding that you seem to be blocked when you try to value yourself? Are you resisting change? Does it just seem to be easier to let people have things for free rather than putting up your prices or telling your clients what your real prices are. This is because you are in your comfort zone and it feels easy to stay where you are.

To step out of your comfort zone is to have the 'difficult or uncomfortable' conversations with your customers about your increase in prices and why. This is all a part of your spiritual journey about speaking up and valuing yourself. Yes, you may lose some clients but you will retain the clients who value you and your services which are the clients you want anyway. The clients who want something for free or at a low price can often be frustrating clients! Do you really want them? Attract clients who value you and what you offer.

Ensure that clients understand the value of working with you. Make them feel that they can't do without you and they will value you and the service that you offer. According to business mentor Ash Lawrence, you do this through offering excellence, consistency, attention to detail, empathy and appreciation within your customer experience.

If you are finding that you just can't value yourself, remember that it is not about you. Remember that you have been given a gift to pass onto the world with your experience and knowledge and it is about serving the people around you with that gift. If I am ever in any doubt about continuing with my work or my business is just feeling too difficult to manage, I just have to remind myself of one thing - 'More people will die, if I don't pass on the experience and knowledge that I have been gifted with'.

I know that I have been gifted with some very deep wisdom which will help many people with depression and chronic ill health. Now I could think selfishly and just do my own thing, but I know deep in my heart that I have to value my wealth of experience and wisdom and pass it on, hence this book, so that I can reach many more people.

Unfortunately, the difficulty of trying to reach those who need my help most and especially those who have self worth issues is that they have told me 'I want to work with you but I can't afford you!', so writing a book is a more cost effective option to reach my potential clients who currently feel that they can't afford to use my services. When they have done the exercises, they will see the value in working with me! Often though I have found that these business owners have had the money, but have not been able to see the value in what I offer as I have not told them how by working with me, they will save money in their business. I have not been specific enough for them to understand what I do and how. Are you doing the same thing?

I had an interesting discussion recently with a therapist who was finding it hard to put her prices up. She said she knew she should, but it just felt awkward. She has one elderly client who is aged 96. She felt it was easier not to mention the price increase to this client, as she never knew if she would see her again. How does she know that the lady isn't going to live to 110! That is 14 years of underpayment. When will she realise that she is worth it!

How well are you valuing others?

If you are not valuing yourself, you will undoubtedly find that your behaviour will not be congruent and you will be pushing away those around you because of your anxious thoughts of not being good enough and being worthy to have them as clients, friends or associates. How well do you value other people's time, gifts and love? Do you turn up late for appointments or forget about your friends until you need them because you are busy or just put your needs first. In 'The Go Giver Sells More' by Bob Burg and John

David Mann, they say 'when you appreciate people, you appreciate and when you don't, you depreciate. You want to increase your own worth - appreciate!'

I've seen all sorts of behaviour when I have been networking with other business owners and there is lots of behaviour where people have lost rapport with me as they have not valued my time, experience and knowledge. Sometimes this has been because I have not valued myself, especially when I was going through a rough patch with depression, but often people just do things which are just bad manners and they don't even realise! Why am I mentioning this now, well every person you talk to is of value and needs to be appreciated and loved. They have a place in society and they often have wisdom to pass on to you. What or who are you ignoring?

When I was at a really low point, I offered to give someone some free lesson observation feedback on one of their nutrition courses which they were launching. It was a genuine offer as I wanted them to do well. I've seen so many courses taught badly and I didn't want them to lose custom and money as they were new to running workshops. I explained to the person that I could not pay to do the course (it just was not a priority for me - a want rather than a need) but that I was happy to attend to help them by giving feedback. I am a leading teacher trainer after all. The person replied that he needed everyone to pay and refused my offer of help. He made me feel terrible and I wished I had never offered.

It massively affected my confidence. He is young and unappreciative and he is clueless about how bad he made me feel. Maybe he will read this book and realise the outcome of his actions.

Whilst I have forgiven him, I now have little inclination to work with him or to put business his way. I just don't need someone like that in my life. This is potentially a big financial mistake for him to make as I am very well connected and anyone who knows me, knows that I happily connect people and help people on a daily basis. You never know who you are talking to or who they are connected to, so be careful to value and appreciate everyone around you.

If you say you are going to do something for someone else, just do it. No matter how little a thing it is. If you have promised to do something, then deliver on your promise. Not delivering is not valuing the other person and this is an indication about how little you value yourself. Trust can be lost between two people very easily and this often happens when one person has not delivered what they said they would.

If you say to a customer, I will ring you back in ten minutes and then don't, you are not valuing them. They maybe by the phone waiting for you. Be really careful in setting achievable expectations for everyone you have dealings with at home and within your business. I write down what I have promised to help me remember. I also set realistic expectations with the person on how quick I can respond as I am often training or delivering therapy.

Have you ever ducked out of an appointment at short notice? It happened to me recently. Someone had booked to see me informally. In fact I had given up part of my day off to help them. Ten minutes after their arrival, their phone rang and said they had to take the call. Their client had turned up a day early and therefore they had to leave.

Now who is not being valued and whose happiness is being put first? The business owner clearly felt that the client had to come first, but surely it was their client's mistake for getting the day wrong of their appointment and they just needed to be reminded that the day was incorrect. My time was not valued as the business owner left and we had to reschedule. The business owner had put the client's happiness ahead of their own which is not valuing them or me!

Valuing your time is all part of your self worth. If you don't value it, who will? Who are you giving too much time too? Do you allow appointments to overrun and not charge your client extra? Do you wait and wait for people to turn up for appointments with you, giving them the benefit of the doubt or do you leave after ten minutes as the person has not valued your time. Time is precious and must not be wasted. Be careful to use your time wisely and that of others.

After every network meeting I attend, I religiously set up connections for the people I have met and send emails/information that I have promised. This takes me time, but I do it willingly as I am valuing the people I have met and building rapport. I love people to say thank you for the connection or the information I have sent, but I am often shocked about how many people don't value the time I have taken by saying a simple 'thank you'. A bit selfish don't you think?

I used to barter a lot in business and I managed to gain a lot of great goods and services in return for me giving therapy or help to another business owner. The problem with this though is that because no money is transferring hands, there can be an issue with both sides seeing the value in each other's services. If you don't feel that you received a good deal, this can affect working together in the future and recommending each other's services. If you are going to barter for services, then you need to ensure that the other person's expectations are properly set and that they understand that they value what they are receiving.

Unfortunately though, people don't value things that they have not paid for. It is a fact, and if you are always trying to barter for everything then you are signalling to the Universe that you will never earn the money you need to pay for the service/goods you require. Start paying for services you receive and value the full service you receive. It is a much stronger energy exchange. You will feel the value much more deeply about what you are receiving.

Exercise:

How are you not valuing yourself now? Be honest...... Who are you putting ahead of your own happiness? What could you do differently?

Additional ways to relax, switch off and to value yourself are:

- ❤ Have a day of just sitting and reading your favourite book/s

- ❤ Spend the day shopping (only if you have the money to do so though)

- ❤ Spend a day at the beach and see how the sea can enhance your energy

- ❤ Spend a day in nature - a wood, near a lake, a country park

- ❤ Organise to have a day or two at a retreat

- ❤ Meditate in your favourite spot for longer than normal

- ❤ Go for a nice walk in the countryside

- ❤ Treat yourself to a lovely meal at your favourite restaurant and enjoy that you are not washing up

- ❤ Spend quality time with your loved ones. Remember time is priceless and even if you don't have money to spend on them, there are lots of free activities where you can be together and connect

- ❤ Value your health and put good quality, unprocessed food into your body and drink plenty of water

- ❤ Spend 10% of the income you earn on yourself and do exactly what you want

7

Are you learning your lessons in life?

'Forget the times of your distress, but never forget
what they taught you.'
Herbert Gasser

What life lessons are you ignoring?

UNTIL NOW, YOU MAYBE didn't even appreciate that you had patterns repeating in life. In Chapter 1, you will have done the exercise of writing down your life history. If you haven't go back to that exercise now and do it as this chapter will make much more sense. You may have thought until now, that the negative stuff that has happened in your life was just what happened. By looking at your past in detail, you will learn so much more which will help you design your life and your business in the way that you want, rather than what you don't want. By looking at your past, you can discover who your ideal client is as your clients will be drawn to you as they know, like and trust you.

For health and wellbeing business owners especially, the traumas you have had in your life, will be the types of issues that you will deal with for your client. My clients for example, often are very quiet and lacking confidence. They find it hard to speak up and be visible in their business off line and online. They usually have a problem with speaking up e.g. doing their pitch or lack confidence to be a speaker. They often suffer from a chronic health condition including depression. They may be experiencing financial difficulties or not able to make a profit from their business due to their lack of self worth. They are often academics or have gained multiple qualifications to feel like they are good enough, but are still struggling in business. Often my clients have had sexual abuse issues too and can feel disconnected from those around them.

For example, you may find by looking at your past, that there is a pattern of rejection in your life. The deepest sense could be that a parent, teacher or friend rejected you when you were young and you learnt at this time to 'expect' others to reject you. I was born at home as an unexpected twin. I was rushed to hospital and spent the first six weeks of my life in an incubator. I felt isolated and lonely in the incubator as I was no longer with my twin and my parents were not there for the whole time.

The deeply sensitive me decided that I had been rejected by my Mum in particular (this was not true), and this definitely affected our relationship throughout our lives. My Mum loved me deeply, but for some reason, I found it difficult to see this and acted as 'you rejected me, so I'll reject you', so whenever she tried to get closer, I repelled. The funny thing was, I was always jealous of my friend's relationships with their Mums, wishing that we were closer. I had no idea that actually I was creating the situation.

By looking at your history, you may discover that this pattern or 'belief' is showing up in your personal and business life. When you go networking, you may find it hard to trust those around you as you are worried that they may reject you or what you are about. You want them to like you, and you are fearful that they will not. With your clients, you are trying really hard to please, so that they don't reject you or at home you may have had a series of personal relationships where either you have bailed out as you are fearful of being hurt and rejected (it felt easier to reject them before they rejected you) or you have expected your partner to go off at some point and they have.

When you are networking, you might be in the habit of expecting others not to like what you do, whether you are a pest controller, a hairdresser or a lawyer. If you are used to saying, 'I'm just a lawyer' and are waiting for someone not to like you or what you do, then this is potentially a pattern linked to where other people have made you believe 'no one likes lawyers'. You may find you say it over and over and it is just the same if you say the thing you do is really boring. Well if it is, why are you doing it?

If you love doing it, then let your passion for what you do and why come out when you are saying your pitch. If you are saying negative things regularly, then this shows that you might be stuck in a pattern. What lessons can you learn from this? What will you say next time you do your pitch?

This is why it is so important to know that your thoughts and feelings are governing everything in your life. The more you resolve the emotional issues in the past and live in the present or 'the now', the easier life will be for you.

When I wrote my history for the first time, I had not realised just how many accidents I had had. It was a bit of an eye opener as another accident after another kept being written down as I remembered. The biggest revelation was that I realised that I had not been happy each time I had an accident and during the time off sick I had (ranging from days to two years), I had used the time to reflect and change career.

According to Louise Hay, one of the probable thoughts I may have had to cause my accident was an inability to speak up. During each accident, I had been struggling to speak up for myself mainly due to issues at work. Strange but true. When the pattern linked to me having accidents was 'fixed' in therapy, it was discovered that subconsciously, I was having accidents 'to get more attention.' As a child, I had learnt that if I hurt myself, I would gain more attention from my parents. I would have set this belief up at an early stage in my life, probably between the ages of 0-8.

The patterns you have in life could well affect how much business you get or not. Within your life, you may have had a history of moving house frequently. It may not have been your fault that this happened. Your parents could have been in the military or just had to move frequently because of work opportunities. Often if you have moved a lot, you can be quite unsettled as a person. You can feel ungrounded. If you have a pattern of feeling unsettled, then you will often have a subconscious belief that 'you will always have to move on again.' This can affect continuity in your business and you also will affect you not making long term friendships. With the need for 'know, like and trust' in networking, this can be a real problem.

Whether your management of money is good or bad will be a pattern too. Are you dealing with your finances or are you being an ostrich? You may be using really bad strategies for managing your finances which need to change.

You always have a choice - Are you wearing the learner or blamer hat?

As mentioned above, you may think life just happens to you and you go through life, not really learning about yourself. As a business owner, you have to start getting into personal development more as your business will not survive if you don't work on yourself and ensure that you look after yourself and believe that you are good enough to have a fantastic profitable business. The more that you learn about yourself and your life, the more you can make the changes you want to achieve the vision you have for your life and business.

Are you the sort of person who takes responsibility or do you look for someone else to blame?

The love game

If you are not loving yourself, you are projecting out that you don't love other people. Perception is projection. What you are thinking is what you are projecting. If you are saying to yourself 'I am deeply loved, I am good enough, I am worthy', you are projecting a message subconsciously to those around you who will be attracted to your positive 'vibe' or energy. You will feel a deeper level of acceptance from others. Like attracts like. As you love yourself more and accept yourself more, and come from a place of love in your life, your energy goes up, your passion is alive and your vision awakens with excitement.

People who want to love you will be attracted to you, including the right clients as they will be inspired by how you can give them the right solution as you have had the problem yourself and solved it. They will 'get you' and want to work with you, as they will be thinking 'well if they can do it, so can I.' You become the leader and they will follow. Your community or audience will surround you. Your client base will increase, as you spend more time with your ideal clients and helping them. You will find it easier to attract your ideal clients to work with you. Of course this works personally as well, so if you are looking for a partner, your chances will go up when you love yourself!

The love game I've designed explains visually how you may be living life as a Learner or a Blamer. Some days you may wake up more negatively and you have to take the Change Lane. By knowing that you have a choice, you can change your life. The most empowered way to live life is with a vision and to act as if you are a learner of your life. The key attributes to have are feeling loved, abundant, being a knower, living in the present and being positive. Being non-judgemental and going with the flow - living life on purpose will bring you great joy.

The Love Game is all about your vision for life and how you are creating your life. Until you wake up and become self-aware, you come from a place of blame rather than learning from your life. When you are a visionary in your life and business, and you 'create' your vision, life lights up for you and you will be so much happier as you realise you can change anything which is not going in the right direction for you. When you have a 'vision' and you like what you see in your life, you will have hope and life will not

THE L♥VE GAME

The happier you feel, the easier it is to create the life you desir

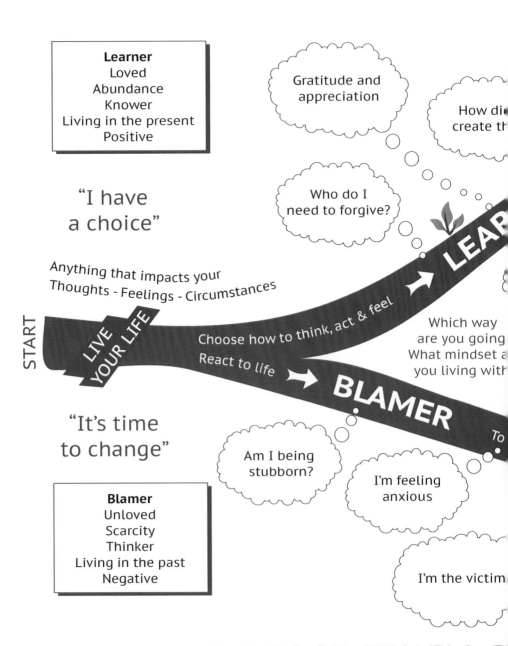

Learner
Loved
Abundance
Knower
Living in the present
Positive

"I have
a choice"

Gratitude and
appreciation

How di
create th

Who do I
need to forgive?

Anything that impacts your
Thoughts - Feelings - Circumstances

START

LIVE
YOUR LIFE

LEAR

Choose how to think, act & feel

React to life

Which way
are you going
What mindset a
you living with

BLAMER

To

"It's time
to change"

Am I being
stubborn?

I'm feeling
anxious

Blamer
Unloved
Scarcity
Thinker
Living in the past
Negative

I'm the victim

TRUST THE UNIVERSE, IT WILL P

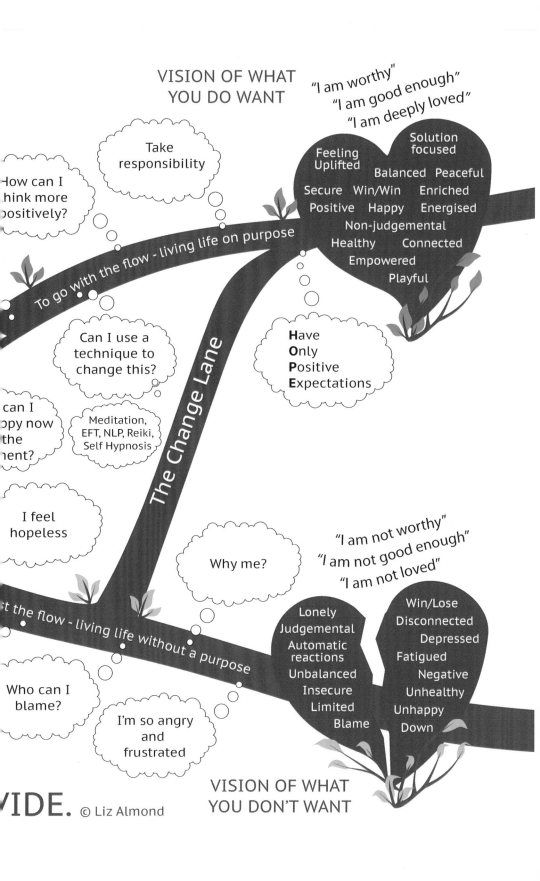

be hopeless and therefore you will not create the emotion of 'hopelessness' within you as you had been doing when you had no 'vision'. You will create more positive emotions such as love, joy, happiness, freedom, gratitude and appreciation.

Be a visionary

By being a visionary, you create what you desire, when you desire it and in a way that you desire it, rather than letting life give you what turns up. You have free will and it is your right to use it, so that you can create a magical life.

Vision stands for:

V   Visionary

I   Intuitive

S   Spiritual

I   Influencer

O   Oracle

N   Networker

Visionary

A business owner must be a visionary within their business, so that they are clear about what they are creating as a business and why. They need to understand the impact of what they are creating (the difference they want to make to the world) and why, for the business to have longevity as this will motivate and empower the business owner. Often business owners are confused about what they are trying to offer and to whom. If they are confused, they will affect the flow of work coming to them and therefore the money that they can earn. They will give off a confused message.

Business owners also need to uncover their values and vision, so that when they outsource work or take on staff, they are recruiting staff in alignment with their values and vision. When you recruit in this way and your team are aligned to your vision and your spiritual mission, they will be happier and understand what role they play in making things happen in your business.

Intuitive

By learning to be intuitive and in alignment with oneself and what is right for you as a business owner, you will know more about what choices you need to make in your business and when. Trusting your intuition and gut and not being overly influenced by others will empower you to continue to help you realise your vision and to create a life you are aspiring to have. It is important for you to speak up and to trust your intuition. By practising regular meditation, an individual will get more in alignment and in tune with who they are as a person and will get more clarity of what they want to achieve. This helps them to be more intuitive.

Anyone who has taken the academic route to achieving qualifications where they have had to use academic writing, may well suffer more stress. The nature of academic writing is that you write about trusted pieces of evidence and then you get to give your opinion. This method teaches you not to trust your own judgement. When you are truly intuitive, you no longer feel the need to have evidence as you know what is right or wrong for you. I often have clients who are academics and their logical, evidenced based side of them, finds it difficult to deal with the more spiritual, less evidence based side and this causes them stress.

Spiritual

When a business owner gets in alignment with their spiritual vision in life which allows them to make a positive difference to the world and they learn to apply spiritual practices, they will get more in flow and they will feel inspired. By getting in alignment with their higher self and meditating around what they want from life and their business, they will be given more inner guidance and wisdom about how to make their dreams happen. Often someone's spiritual mission can be so powerful inside, this can be difficult to express as it can feel so big.

For example, inside your mind, you are being shown you are a global healer like myself on a humanitarian mission to help millions of individuals. I found it incredibly difficult to tell everyone how I was feeling, what I was thinking and I didn't know how to articulate my knowledge so that I was understood. I was worried that people would think I was mad. When I finally let go and trusted, I was able to write this book and there are more books on their way.

When you are unable to be at one with your spiritual mission or you are unclear about what your purpose and mission is, this can show up as anger, anxiety, depression and exhaustion in your life. You will feel unfulfilled. It is so important to feel fulfilled by your life and to live your life on purpose. You may also be acting as an empath and taking on board other people's emotions and this is behaviour that you must change for the sake of your own health and to help more people. You need to desensitise by learning how to relate to those around you differently.

Influencer

Depending on the spiritual mission you are on, it will probably mean that within your business you need to influence others effectively when you are networking, or trying to attract your clients. Your communication skills are key to making this work effectively for you. Often, I have met business owners who are very angry or annoyed at others or who are trying to influence others in the wrong way.

For example, at a network event I meet a tree consultant. I was intrigued as I had never met one before. I asked more questions to find out more about his business and how I could help him. He said he would like to be introduced to property developers and then started to talk very negatively about developers and the fact that they weren't interested in saving the trees when developing/building properties.

He was so negative, I wasn't sure I wanted to connect him with any of my contacts! I explained to him that all the property developers I know were lovely and would definitely care about protecting the environment and would like to know more. I also spent time explaining why he wasn't influencing me well by his argument and why. He soon got the message. He was so passionate about saving trees, he hadn't realised he had to 'educate and influence' his clients and those interested in his network about why trees needed to be saved and not put anger behind his argument! Love is always the key!

Oracle

Whether you have a business or not, it is now recommended that you make a decision to create passive income in your life to top up your income whether that is supplementing your main salary or your pension. Passive income, is income that you earn without being actively involved. That usually means that you continue to make income with no or very little effort on your part to maintain that cash flow. You can do this whether you are aged 12 or 80! A part time business on the side, will allow you more freedom to live the lifestyle you want to create and you do this by monetising your wisdom and becoming an oracle.

Every business owner has a gift and enlightened wisdom that they can share with others. This might be to help save the planet, feel better, empower someone to fell happier or they might be sharing a system or process for something which can be done more easily. This wisdom can be packaged in some way and can be sold on as passive income in the form of e-books, e-courses, and books or oracle cards. The wisdom can by systemised (remember 'VISION' which is a part of my 'VISIONary' system). This helps you to write blog posts, newsletters, social media content etc and share your wisdom more easily for your own clients or 'tribe' and for people to buy from you.

The final element of being an oracle is public speaking and sharing your wisdom. Not only can you sell through the room but you can make a massive impact through what you say depending on who is in the room. This will give you sales and connections. By speaking from the heart about your wisdom and sharing your knowledge will empower and enlighten others. By being the Oracle, you are sharing your wisdom for the greater good and not hiding and you will also make more sales as you will be seen as an expert in your field which will bring you more opportunities. Of course, you could just share your knowledge for free if money isn't a problem by giving talks and inspiring others through it.

Networker

Manifesting profitable connections when networking can create you endless referrals of work for years to come, however it is essential that you learn the correct networking skills or else you can be deflecting potential business without even realising. It is essential that you understand that the primary aim of networking is not to seek business but to bring happiness to another person. As you give to another – advice, gifts, wisdom, friendship, support etc, you will receive love back. Provided you have identified who your ideal client is and are clear about what you offer as a business, you will receive help back, even years after you have helped them.

By building know/like/trust when building relationships with others you met, you will create trusted connections with others which will empower your business and personal life towards success and profitability. Building relationships over years, will enable you to gain support when you need it and referrals.

You have choices

The choices you make will empower and enlighten your life. Remember you have free will. It is your choice how you choose to create your life.

Choices stands for:

C   Circumstances

H   Hope/Heart/Health

O   Opportunities

I   Intuition/Intent

C   Change

E   Empowered/Enlightened

S   Strength/Security

Circumstances

The circumstances you find yourself within your business or in your personal life which affect your business life can sometimes seem overwhelming and disempowering. Circumstances can seem a lot worse than we think they are because we overthink things. Remember that by seeing the good in a situation (the hidden blessings) and feeling gratitude, we can make a situation which first seemed grim into something much better. Your emotional state affects your perception of circumstances, so always try to see the positive in what can seem to be a negative situation.

For example, you might be heart broken that your daughter is leaving home. She is your confidante and you are going to miss her. The hidden blessing is that you will have more time to spend with your partner and to get to re-kindle your relationship with them. You will be able to get into the bathroom quicker and you won't find that your make up has disappeared into your daughter's room. You may also have been subconsciously overprotecting your daughter too, and this is a time to let her grow and to spread her wings and to gain more confidence.

Hope/Heart/Health

Having Only Positive Expectations (HOPE) in your life is much kinder on your heart. Your heart will feel lighter and brighter. As you love yourself more, by having hope and not being angry and hopeless, you will see more opportunities in life. Always aspire to having the attitudes of gratitude, positivity and success by having a happy heart. As shown, in the Love Game, knowing that you are worthy, good enough and deeply loved is key. You achieve this by loving life, living your life on purpose rather than thinking life has dealt you a bad hand.

Your heart is so powerful, in fact according to the Heart Maths Institute www.heartmath.org, your heart is 5000 more powerful than your mind. Working towards having a happy heart and doing what you love, will lead you to better health and happiness. Remember your health is your wealth. Work towards getting your heart and head in alignment and you will have an empowered and enlightened life and of course money will be more plentiful.

Opportunities

Opportunities open doors but often we close doors without realising we are doing it. When you feel unhappy, often you will isolate yourself from friends and family. You will avoid social gatherings and talking to others. For example, when negative things happen in your business, you can feel embarrassed or worried. You start to dis-connect from others. You may do this by not phoning someone when you know you should or by deliberately not attending functions where you could get business.

By focusing more on choosing to be happy and being grateful for what you have, you will receive more opportunities. When you help others and become less self-focused, the Universe will provide you with even more positive opportunities. The choice is yours, always take opportunities as they occur if it feels right to do so and always listen to your intuition.

Intention/Intuition

Willpower is key when you are looking to change yourself. It is really important that you set the intention to change. By 'intending' to do something, you are expecting it to happen. You are getting the energy flowing. Intend to change, by telling others and showing that you are serious about the change. Make yourself accountable to someone – a coach or trusted friend so that you really take action to change and you don't chicken out of it. Most importantly, your intention should be recorded in a written format as you are setting the change in you as if it was set in stone.

By following your intuition, you will know what is right for you to change and when. You may intuitively feel resistance to making changes in your personal and business life. As mentioned before, daily meditation will help you get into flow, will help you understand what actions to take and you will intuitively make the changes you need to make in your life, by following the internal guidance you are given via your higher self.

Choice/Change

You always have a choice in life to change your insights, thoughts and circumstances. It may not feel that way at the time, but it is true, when you become fully aware that you are creating your own reality, you can change how you are thinking, feeling and reacting to situations in your life and business. It may mean doing something new which feels a little scary, but that is probably because you have been stubbornly stuck in your comfort zone for too long. Everyone needs to grow towards fulfilling their potential and their energy within us needs to be able to flow not be stuck.

Our bodies are full of emotions – positive and negative and they need to flow. Remember e-motion means – 'energy in motion'. If you take on board other people's pain or emotion, then you are using your empathic qualities in the wrong way and need to learn new ways to become emotionally detached but still empathic so that you have more energy and can help more people. You have to choose to make this change. If you are too stubborn about moving out of your comfort zone, you will get stuck! Knee and neck pain often relate to being too stubborn.

Empowered/Enlightened

By taking control of your life and how you react to it means that you will naturally become more empowered. By analysing what is going on in each experience you are having, you are becoming even more self-aware and enlightened. When we let go of negative emotions and experiences from our past, our bodies actually 'feel' lighter. Heavy burdens lift and we have more energy. Negative emotion is heavy and can keep us stuck often in fear or anxiety. It felt as though I was walking through treacle when I was depressed. As we lift the negative heavy emotions, positive emotions which are lighter can flow.

Underneath the physical body, is your energetic body and aura and as you learn techniques such as Reiki, Emotional Freedom Technique, Self-Hypnosis and Meditation, you can remove what is stuck. The energy body is made up of energy points called Chakras and these Chakras relate to different aspects of our life. There is a shaft of light running through the Chakras from the top of your head through to your feet. As we learn a lesson in life or remove a 'block' of dark negative energy from our body, our body will get physically lighter and we can also 'see' more light behind our eyes and we feel more empowered and enlightened.

Strength/Security

Your inner strength is much stronger that you think. Often you can believe that you are weak and a victim in situations. Actually, everyone has the inner resources to change how they are feeling and reacting to life. If you are saying negative thoughts to yourself, you will weaken your body. For example, if you say 'I can't do this' or 'it's not possible' or 'I'm weak and unable' your body will react in accordance to this.

Start saying powerful words to yourself such as 'I am strong', 'I am powerful' and notice how strong and powerful you become. If you say these statements, but don't believe them, this shows you have an underlying limiting belief which you need to address. Always say strong affirmations to give you strength. Getting though negative situations is challenging and you will have the strength if you dig deep. You have the inner resources and you are worth it!

Feeling secure is very important to you and by trusting the Universe to provide, will give you security. When you are not trusting, you will feel more insecure. As mentioned before, if you don't take responsibility about money, you will produce the emotion of 'insecurity' in your body which will give you more anxiety. Always work towards giving yourself a good foundation in anything you are going to do. For example, if your financial circumstances are really poor, one thing to do to make you feel more secure, is to spend time with your partner looking at your finances together, so that you are both clear about how to move forward for the future.

You have wealth already

Wealth isn't just the money you physically have in the bank. It is linked to your environment, nature, opportunities, friends and family and having fun and your interaction with these things. Life is a gift and is so much more than money.

Wealth stands for:

W Wisdom

E Emotional Health

A Acceptance of Self

L Learner

T Thoughts

H Healing

Wisdom

Your inner wisdom and gifts need to be cherished. Everyone is wise, but often because of our 'not good enough' messaging we don't realise what value is actually within us. Whether you have a business or not, you are a wise person and you have knowledge which needs to be shared with others.

When we don't appreciate our value and wisdom, we make mistakes, we don't trust our intuition and believe that other people know best. We bow to the belief of another and don't say what we mean in line with our wisdom. This can leave you angry and frustrated when you are living from the limiting belief of 'I can't speak up' as I was. The negative emotion within can be overwhelming of not being able to share what you truly know to be true.

If you are a business owner, you must monetise your wisdom to increase your wealth and create passive income products/services based on your unique wisdom. This could be a book, an e-course, journal or a set of oracle cards. If you are not a business owner, I would still encourage you do this. As pensions are now not so secure, feeding your retirement fund with passive income is now a sensible option as you will always be able to afford what you want to achieve and experience within your retirement.

Emotional Health

To be able to create the wealth you are creating in your life, you need to have a handle on your emotions and understand how they link to you manifesting what you want in life. Positive emotions such as love, joy, gratitude, freedom and appreciation give you a higher 'vibe' or 'vibration'. If you have negative emotions such as anger, resentment, sadness, guilt, hopelessness, despair or loneliness will give you a negative 'vibe'. The

The Positive and Negative Emotional Scale of Health, Wealth and Happiness

A Happy Heart – Loving, Light, Positive, Grateful, Alkaline

Passion, Joy, Happiness, Love, Delight, Appreciation, Gratitude
Empowered, Enlightened, Abundant, Freedom, Optimist
Peace of Mind, Serenity, Calm, Stability
Hope, Contentment, Success, Fulfilment
Achievement, Security, Strength, Confidence
Excitement, Enthusiasm, Eagerness

An Unhappy Heart – Unloving, Dark, Negative, Ungrateful, Acidic

Unfulfilled, Bored, Miserable, Stubborn, Lonely, Irritated
Disrespected, Impatient, Annoyed, Pessimist, Overwhelmed
Anxious, Doubt, Distrust, Regret, Disappointment
Grief, Sadness, Frustration, Greed
Anger, Guilt, Hurt, Jealousy, Blame, Insecurity, Unworthiness
Hopeless, Depression, Powerless, Helpless, Resentment, Hatred
Despair, Shame, Fear, Rejection, Sorrow

negative emotions are toxic to the body and if left in the body, they will eventually lead to illness and dis-ease (read 'You can heal your life' by Louise Hay). Stress is toxic to your body and you want to always be finding ways to release your stress or dis-ease and to be more relaxed and at ease with yourself.

Your health is your wealth, and if you want to earn more money, it needs to be your sole mission to remove negative emotions from your body by changing your thoughts, feelings and behaviour to be more positive. Value yourself and your body. Negative emotions are dark and heavy and you want your body to be light and bright and to be energised. Work away from being acidic and judgemental and become alkaline and non judgemental. Live in the present with love, laughter, and joy.

Actions

The actions you take towards and away from earning your wealth is key. As you know, from the Law of Attraction, you have to ask for what you want, believe it is possible and you will receive it as well as taking inspired action. If you don't take enough action or you are too negative and heavy with negative emotion, you will not be able to manifest what you want to attract whether this is money, more customers or other material possessions such as a car or a house.

Planning your actions and keeping the end goal in sight will help you achieve the wealth you are hoping to achieve. Write down your actions in a business plan (including what you are hoping to achieve personally) and you will have success. The Universe needs your actions to be journaled in some way, so that it knows how to help you.

Lessons

Learning lessons from your life is key to building the wealth you are looking for in your life. The three main areas you need to focus on when it comes to learning lessons are about your health, wealth, and happiness.

For example, you may not be in a positive position with your business right now. You may have become ill through the stress of not making as much profit as you hoped and you are feeling a bit depressed and hopeless about turning things around. There are lessons in here about needing to have an attitude of success, gratitude, and positivity. You may need to learn to look after your body and learn new stress relief techniques to release the stress. If you don't exercise at the moment and never stop doing business focussed activities, there will be lessons to learn about 'being' not 'doing' as well as educating your mind about alternative methods to release anxiety/pain other than taking a pill or visiting your doctor.

There may be lessons about switching from being a 'loner' to a 'learner' in your life, becoming more self-aware and hopeful for the future. Remember your health is your wealth. What wealth lessons do you need to be learning about managing money, being positive about money and also in changing your anxieties towards money if you are money phobic?

By learning lessons, issues which affected you in the past will disappear or reduce in significance. It will allow you to live in the present and to get more in flow within your life with far less resistance.

To learn a wealth lesson, often you have to look very closely at your money behaviour. It might be that you are not taking responsibility for your debt. Are you burying your head in the sand and hoping that the issue will go away? Financial planning, budgeting and learning about how to manage and communicate about your finances with others is key to your success. This means that you have taken ownership and you will start feeling more empowered about money as you understand it better.

Thoughts

The thoughts you are having need to always be positive. Past experiences may have taught you to think negatively though and coloured your view on life. You may be very judgemental about yourself and others as I was. It is your job now to spot what you are saying to yourself and to reframe it in your mind to something more positive. Remember about the Law of Attraction and all the attractive qualities you have to have to get it to work. You are creating your own reality from your thoughts.

If you are thinking negatively about a lack of money or profit, you will attract this. Think about ways to make money, see in your mind making money and take inspired action and see new wealth as much more than just the physical money you have in your purse. Loving yourself is all a part of wealth.

Healing

The more anxious you become about not having money and the more you don't take action to heal yourself about your negative thinking about money, the more likely you are to find yourself in debt or attract issues where you have to pay out more money e.g. unexpected bills, equipment breaking down, etc.

When you take action to heal an issue within you e.g. dyslexia or dyscalculia, you start to heal yourself. You learn lessons through healing yourself and by taking on board new thoughts, feelings, and beliefs. Issues will resolve themselves. If you ignore issues, you are ignoring the opportunity to heal yourself and what is going on in your life.

It is important to use the Love Game at all times in your life to help you remember that you always want to be spotting any aspect of you which relates to your health, wealth, and happiness which has a negative perspective. By healing these issues, you will have a happier, healthier, and wealthier life and you will have more longevity of life too as you are living from the right attitudes – positivity, gratitude, and success.

Remember that your health is your wealth and a happy life will give you greater wealth and happiness. In business or just life generally, you may have off days or need to move out of your comfort zone and it is therefore appropriate to apply a technique such as Reiki, NLP, EFT or self hypnosis, which is why I teach these skills as they help you get back into alignment and overcome anxiety and other negative emotions.

If you live life as a Blamer, you will be less compassionate to yourself and others and will be judging life more harshly. You will be more judgemental, and will be going against the flow of life and without a purpose or vision. The clients I work with, have often been living like this for some time and there is usually a sense of depression or unhappiness which we need to work on, on a one to one basis to transform their current behaviour of being a Blamer, feeling unloved, living from scarcity, being a thinker, living in the past and being more negative. It is such a joy to see them transform from being a Blamer to becoming a Learner of their life as most people don't realise that there is a different way.

Trusting the Universe to provide is essential to gaining the life you desire. You can create anything you wish for. It may not come in the way that you expected, but you can manifest from your thoughts anything you desire including money. You just have to believe that it is possible.

Traits to watch out for

Trust is key. If you are having anxious thoughts, this means you have a high level of the feeling of distrust within you. This will relate to an issue in your past which needs to be resolved. In Louise Hay's book 'You can heal your life', she found that anxiety was 'not trusting the process and flow of life'. By fixing trust issues and having positive thoughts, you will naturally feel more secure.

By ensuring that you send love to yourself, your network and the rest of the world in your meditations, you are helping to heal your heart and to open your heart chakra. As your heart remains open and your energy increases, you will find it easier to spread your wings in business. This depends on what you are visioning for and what you have identified in your business plan. The number of clients you can reach and help will depend on the strategies you are applying and how well you are projecting in your mind what you want to receive.

It is possible to get frustrated that you have a gift to offer people, but you may not have the opportunities you would like to help people exactly as you want. Remember, if you are a perfectionist, it is especially important that you reframe your thinking about lowering your standards as you are judging yourself harshly and you will find your lower standards are still higher than everyone else's. The self criticism you give yourself is unjustified and is unloving behaviour towards yourself. Your high standards stops it being easy to release control of aspects of your business, as you feel no one else can do it as well as you. This therefore causes you more stress as your business grows.

Training others to understand and value your standards and systems, will enable you to relax and trust others to help you with your business and will in the long run make you more money.

Are you being stubborn about something? Do you feel stuck? Often stubbornness is the reason. It may be time to look at your thinking more deeply to see if you are really flexible with your thinking or are you the sort of person who has lots of black and white thoughts? Do you see many options in your mind, or do you just have a choice of this or that? Remember energy needs to flow. If you are stopping yourself in some way, resisting change for example or not letting someone help you (a poor receiver), stubbornness is often the cause. Are you being flexible enough with your thoughts or are they too rigid?

To gain the most out of life, it is to live your life on purpose by going with the flow. When you are fighting the flow you are living your life without purpose and vision. You are supposed to live your life and you do have a choice. You can choose how to think, act and feel or you can react to life and act as the Blamer, judging yourself and others negatively.

Do you naturally practise kindness? You may find it an odd question but the kindness you show others will come back to you. I am a great believer of what goes around, comes around. I help hundreds of people and love doing so and every day I am rewarded in different ways for my kindness. You can start small by offering a smile to someone and brightening their day or you can go bigger and pay for others to achieve success or donate money to charity if you can afford to do so.

Are you being congruent in your business? Desire, belief and self-esteem all need to be in alignment to get the best results. It is very powerful when you have all three aspects flowing in the same direction. I regularly meet business people who confess to me that they don't practise their own advice. This can really affect your reputation if you are not practising what you preach. I often work with business owners to re-programme their beliefs so

Exercise:

What patterns do you recognise in your life which keep happening to you around money? Do you choose to react to things that happen to you around money or do you learn from the experience?

that they are not sabotaging in this way. This self-sabotage is really common and is often linked to a fear of success or failure.

You may feel disconnected from those around you. Often if you have had a bad day, you cannot face talking to anyone. If you have a series of bad days, and you again avoid talking to friends or family, one of your habits may be to 'disconnect' from those around you. Another reason for this is to protect yourself from really feeling your feelings as they are too painful. It may well be a life lesson to 'reconnect' with people around you, which means that you have to learn how to speak up and communicate with others once again. It also means that you have to help others and ask for help which may also not be your usual pattern.

Those who decide to train in Reiki with me, are being re-connected spiritually to their source energy and the feedback I am given following their empowerment is that they feel a deeper sense of peace and fulfilment by doing so.

If you are lacking in money, then you may be missing opportunities to make money because of this behaviour. For example, you may not want to go networking to meet other business owners as you are fearful of getting to know people and telling them about what you do. I know I went through this journey. I used to look at people at a network, and I felt disconnected. I used to think 'how will I fit in?' Everyone looked like they knew everyone and the anxiety within me was off the scale. However, it was vital for my business that I relaxed and told people about what I did to promote myself and my services to get business. I love networking now and I walk into the room and it is like meeting lots of friends and it is a lot of fun.

In the book, The One Minute Millionaire it pulls this concept together by saying 'getting your act together is the final key to manifesting what you want in your life.'

8

The power of gratitude

'Joy is an attitude; it is the presence of love - for self and others. It comes from a feeling of inner peace, the ability to give and receive and appreciation of self and others. It is a state of gratitude and compassion, a feeling of connection to your higher self.'

Unknown

When you think about 'gratitude' what do you think it really means? Who do you need to be grateful to and why? I used to think - I'm very polite. I'd always say thank you when I had been given something or send thank you cards, but that is the logical answer rather than the spiritual answer to this question. I was thanking people for material things, and objects, rather than appreciating and valuing what I already had in life such as my health, my family, nature surrounding me and the relationships I had with other people. Often I was not appreciating what I already had in life such as the fact that I can see out of both my eyes, walk as far as I want, I had freedom to go wherever I wanted, and I had many possessions which brought me pleasure.

Of course, I was missing the greatest thing to be grateful for which was the fact that I can breathe and I am alive! When you feel deep gratitude in your heart for the specifics of life, you are thanking your source energy, God, your creator, whoever you think brought you to this planet. Funnily enough, the more grateful you become, life just gets better and better, so why aren't people using such a free and simple technique is a wonder as it works when you focus on appreciating the money you have in the bank, what you spend and what you have already spent money on such as your possessions and experiences. Wake up the spirit within you and focus on your passion and be grateful for what you have. See how your life changes for the better.

The late motivational guru Wayne Dyer says 'Without exception, begin every day of your life with gratitude. As you look in the mirror, say, "Thank you, God, for life, for my body, for my family and loved ones, for this day, and for the opportunity to be of service. Thank you, thank you, thank you!" If you are not religious, there is no need to worry. God is whoever you think it is. The power of the Universe which created you.

Appreciation is the key to your success

Often we can believe that we are only successful when we 'have' something. This can be when we have achieved a qualification, a possession or even a person. We often are striving for success (not feeling good enough) and in doing so are missing the very essence of life. We are going too fast through life, not appreciating being 'in the moment' as we are emotionally charged by our past or are living a life of being anxious about our uncertain future.

When we slow down and increase our awareness of our surroundings, the people in our lives and our possessions and start to appreciate them and feel grateful for them, we begin to realise just how much we do have. A lot of the materialistic things our egos may feel we need and therefore need to finance will disappear. When we actually 'stop', we notice so much more. The beauty of what is around us. In essence, this is being mindful. You need to train yourself from being in the 'doing mode' to be in the 'being mode'.

According to Mark Williams and Danny Penman, in their book 'Mindfulness - a practical guide to finding peace in a frantic world', there are seven characteristics of 'doing' and being' modes of minds.

Doing	Being
Automatic pilot	Conscious choice
Analysing	Sensing
Striving	Accepting
Seeing thoughts as solid and real	Treating thoughts as mental events
Avoidance	Approaching
Mental time travel	Remaining in the present moment
Depleting	Nourishing activities

The key is to move yourself from being in the 'doing' mode to be in the 'being' mode at all times. You do have a choice, but you might not have realised this until now. In their excellent book, 'Change your questions, change your life', Marilee Adams has created a choice map exercise to show how you can choose at any one moment how to be in life - A learner or judger. If you are living your life as a judger, then you will end up in the judger pit which is depression and chronic ill health.

The more that you learn from how you react to life and make conscious choices, you can improve your life and become happier. You need to sense what is going on around you and within your body and trust your intuition as it is always right. You need to be accepting of what is going on and know that thoughts in your mind can just disappear as quickly as they arrived.

By approaching anything with a positive expectation, you will receive a more positive result and this comes from living in the present moment, rather than the past or the future in your mind. By carrying out nourishing activities such as meditating, exercising, walking, listening to music, dancing or reading you will be feeding your soul, rather than depleting it by watching depressing news articles, gossiping about colleagues and worrying about what might not happen.

If you are interested in learning more about mindfulness meditation, then visit my website at www.insightfulminds.co.uk.

Appreciating what you already have and valuing it

Appreciating what you already have and valuing it is essential. Things like our health, our family, our friends, possessions and of course the beauty of nature need to be remembered and appreciated. So often we can be negative about things in our lives which then cause us more problems.

For example, you may not notice when you get home that your wife has tidied your house whilst you were at work. You still have the stressful day at the office in the forefront of your mind. If you chose to say something negative to your wife such as 'why is my dinner not ready yet?' and totally forget to say thank you for tidying up, you are not showing appreciation and gratitude for your partner.

Often this is what happens when one partner works and the other stays home with the kids. There can be an expectation that the partner at home is not working and therefore when things like tidying up or the dinner are not ready, there is a lack of appreciation for how much effort it takes to keep children entertained. Your partner will feel unappreciated and will potentially become more distant. Appreciation builds love, trust and connection between others.

Be honest with yourself. By being honest, you can start to make changes to ensure that you are more grateful for what or who you have in your life. Appreciating people, possessions and everything you have in life, will allow you to feel happier and remove negative emotion that you have been previously creating.

Exercise:

What are you not appreciating in your life? Who do you need to appreciate more and why?

Do you not have as much money as you would like?

When you feel that you do not have enough money in your life, you start to focus on the 'lack' of money. This might be because you can't find the money to fund an aspect of your business or you are feeling guilty that you can't take your family away on holiday, as there is a lack of cash flow in your business. For those of you in debt who are reading this book, you may be feeling the pressure of it and therefore you may find that your mind dwells on the happy times in your past when you did have money, and when you reflect on how things are now, you may start focussing on lack which then can cause you greater anxiety.

As mentioned in Chapter 1, Rhonda Byrne from 'The Secret' says 'think more thoughts in a day of abundance than a lack of money.' Remove the need to focus on a lack of money in your life and appreciate what you do have. It is a gift to be alive, to be able to read, dance, have fun, to have sex, and to be playful. By appreciating attributes such as these, you will help retrain your mind to see all the positives in your life, rather than what is not going right.

When I was suffering from a lack of money, I was really stressed. I applied so much pressure to myself to succeed and achieve with my business. The thing is, if you are stressed and anxious, you will be pushing away the ability to earn money as the stress is making you ill and is creating negative emotions in the body such as anger, loneliness, fear, anxiety, hopelessness and depression. These emotions make it much harder to manifest money. Appreciate what you do have, even if it is only 2p in your bank account and remain positive. Things can change in an instant. Belief in yourself is essential.

Raise your vibe and stop focusing on money

We can focus so much on money that we miss all the small things in life which we take for granted. For example, the clothes we are wearing, that we have a safe place to live or we can easily escape into the countryside to have a day out with our family that is free! Whilst money is a need, there are hundreds of things that you can do for free which will raise your 'vibe'. You can go for a walk, enjoy a hot bath, or enjoy a little intimate time with your partner. Appreciating the small positives in life, helps you deal with the challenges.

According to Rhonda Byrne in her book, 'The Magic', one very quick way to raise your vibe, is to walk 100 steps saying thank you at every step. Just notice how much more positive you feel once you have done this. I often do this when walking my dog Charlie to help me to focus on the beauty around me. It also clears the mind too as you can't focus on anything except saying 'thank you'.

Remember, if you are feeling low or unhappy, you need to aspire to get yourself happier. Use the Emotional Scale of Health, Wealth and Happiness as your guide in chapter 7. Ask yourself, 'How am I feeling?', acknowledge the emotion you are feeling e.g. loneliness and use a technique such as meditation, Reiki, self hypnosis or Emotional Freedom Technique to release this negative emotion in you.

Appreciating money which has been spent on us

How often do you go through a day spending money and not even noticing what you spent it on or what things cost? This is showing a lack of appreciation and respect for the money in our possession. We spend it without thinking as it is so easy for money to come out of our accounts as direct debits, contactless payments and just because we are too busy to notice! Every time I spend money, in my head, I say 'thank you for the money' and feel gratitude that I can pay for an item. The more you do this, the more it becomes an unconscious habit. By showing more gratitude for what you have bought, you are valuing the items more. You are recognising the blessings of the ability to be able to earn your own money and spend it, as many people in the world do not have this luxury.

When we have bought an item, for example a new car, how well do you look after it? Do you leave all your rubbish in it, week after week or are you meticulous about cleaning it inside and out? Did you know that your car represents your energy field and your life, so if you are trashing it every day by throwing litter all over it, you are not respecting your life. Keep it clean and clear and just notice how much clearer your thinking is. The exact same thing applies to your home. A tidy, uncluttered home relates to a tidy and clear thinking mind.

Valuing your possessions, makes them last. We are a throwaway society. We don't appreciate what we have bought and often people buy things and then start criticising them for not being good enough as soon as they have bought them. Children often don't appreciate their Christmas presents as they are given so much these days. The money spent on children has often got out of hand, which can be an added pressure to you as parents. Children learn to look for the next gift to unwrap rather than appreciating one special gift.

Our need to compare with others often gets triggered at this point too, especially if other family members spend more than you do on presents.

Having suffered the anxiety of being in debt, I would wholeheartedly recommend that you do not go into debt when buying presents for your family and children. Set a good example. Buying a small gift which means something to the recipient is far more meaningful and will be remembered.

Becoming more aware of what you have bought and looking more consciously about how to save money when you are buying things, will show the Universe that you are respecting money and are appreciating it.

Exercise:

Reflect right now about all the times in the past when you have spent money or money has been spent on you. There will be lots of times when you have not appreciated the flow of money in your life. It could be as simple as when your parents bought you an ice cream when you were on your summer holidays aged three or paying for your newspaper with your contactless credit card when you were rushing for a train.

In your mind, there is a timeline of events which have happened to you, go back to your earliest memory, and say 'thank you' for the money being spent and then continue saying thank you for all the memories of when money has flowed into your life which come up on your timeline until now. Take your time on this and feel deep heartfelt gratitude that you have had the money in your life. Often we are deeply ungrateful around money and disrespect it, which is why this exercise is so powerful. Every time you spend money in the future or money is spent on you, ensure you feel gratitude. This will help change your relationship with money.

Appreciating and valuing what other people do for us

How many times have you helped someone from your network of business contacts and they have not said 'thank you' or shown enough appreciation of your help. How does it feel not to be thanked? It is so lovely to have recognition for the help we have given. Saying thank you properly, feels good and makes the other person feel valued. We all get so busy, it is easy to forget, but you might not be so flippant about forgetting when you realise the deeper impact of not saying 'thank you' in a meaningful way. Some personality types really crave recognition for the help they give and if they are not thanked or the thanks they receive is a bit shallow, they can become resentful and will be less likely to help you again in the future.

I am known in my network for sending handmade cards. I genuinely love creating them and ensuring the other person who has helped me knows how grateful I am for them helping me. Anyone can just say 'thank you', but giving or sending something which is personalised, can mean so much more to a person. I haven't always been in a position financially to buy a gift, but when I can, or see something special I know a networking friend will like, I will buy it. I know I am remembered because I have helped people and this also means that if I need help from someone in my network, they will be more likely to want to help me.

Appreciation attracts appreciation. I know that I can call on someone I have helped and they will help me, even if it is in a few years time. What I find fascinating is when people don't say 'thank you' or even notice what effort you have gone to to help them. Being taken for granted by someone in your network can feel bad and can affect relationships greatly. If someone in your network has helped you, ensure you thank them openly in front of others or on social media. Give them testimonials which will help their business too on Facebook, Linked in and Twitter. Be careful not to promise to do this and then forget to do it!

Daily gratitude affirmations

By saying at least ten gratitudes 'thank yous' per day, you will raise your positive vibe, which will make it easier to manifest the money you desire in your life. To be honest, I say 'thank you' to myself at least 100 times a day if not more. I say 'thank you' for specific things I have received everyday, whether that is a fantastic testimonial, a gift, seeing a fabulous sunset, being able to spend money or just that I am thanking myself for being me! My friend Emma Cook of the Tranquility Room says her top gratitudes for every day are as follows:

- ❤ I am grateful of the world and it's magic, thank you, thank you, thank you.....

- ❤ I am grateful of the people in my life, thank you, thank you, thank you.....

- ❤ I am grateful of bad times as they make me appreciate good times, thank you, thank you, thank you.....

- ❤ I am grateful of my body and it's ability to get me through the day with little to no appreciation for the magical ways it works, thank you, thank you, thank you.....

- ❤ I am grateful of my good health, thank you, thank you, thank you.....

Blessings in disguise

Often people say to me when they are feeling down or unhappy about situations that they just can't see a positive in it. They are so blinkered by the negative, they can't see the positive. By looking for the blessings in disguise for the situation you are in, you will learn to remove the negativity out of a situation. For example, your husband may have left you and you are really angry and hurt by how he has treated you. The blessings in disguise maybe that you have had three wonderful children or that you moved areas to get married again which allowed you to find your perfect job.

Being grateful for the good times, helps you to get through the bad times. Reminders of the past are anchored in our minds. We have pictures in our minds of positive and negative experiences and by seeing the blessings in disguise when something is not going our way, we can release the negative and let it go. We need to live in the present and not the past, and by saying gratitudes to yourself every day, allows you to release the negative charge.

You may wish to invest in a gratitude journal to write down your gratitudes each day or have a special jar where you add a gratitude message every time something great happens. To learn more about gratitude and its positive effects read 'The Magic' by Rhonda Byrne. Every evening, I write in a journal about all the positive aspects of my day. I note down what I received and what I appreciated and am grateful for.

Using the law of attraction and gratitude

For the Law of Attraction to work on your desires, you must be visualising the item of your desire as if you have it now and are feeling a sense of deep gratitude that you can have it. By feeling gratitude, you are signalling to the Universe that you are ready to receive what you have asked for. Appreciation allows the magic to happen in your life. Try it out and see.

Before I require something (big or small), I say to myself 'thank you, thank you, thank you for _____' This works in helping me to find a parking space, the right clients, the right connections for my business, as well as when something goes wrong for me. For example, I might turn on my laptop and the screen is blank. Rather than panic and go into melt down, I calmly say 'Thank you, thank you, thank you, for my laptop now functioning without a problem.' It then works.

Anxiety and negative thoughts will never fix your problems. Being calm, relaxed and positive will. Clearly you have to have ultimate faith or belief that something will change for you because if you don't you are giving off a negative thought. You will be surprised what will change or turn up in your life when you use this technique. I've sorted out a whole range of issues linked to general life and my financial situation and I practise this technique regularly.

9

Forgive to forget

'If you haven't forgiven yourself something,
how can you expect to forgive others?'
Dolores Huerta

WHO HAVE YOU NOT forgiven? Has something happened in the past to make you resent another? Have you 100% forgiven others? I always remember being sat in my friend's café listening to a customer describe something her daughter had done and saying 'I'll never, ever forgive her for that.' Ek.... This is not a good plan or strategy for life. If you hold onto any resentment or can't forgive someone, in fact it is yourself who you can't forgive.

The mind is a projector of your thoughts. You are thinking them and you are judging another if you think someone has done something bad to you. The best plan is when you feel someone has done something you don't like, send loving thoughts to it and learn from the experience as it might be one of your lessons in life as described in Chapter 7. If you have not forgiven someone from your past, you will still be linking to your past emotionally and therefore not living in the present.

Forgive others by forgiving yourself

According to Money Mindset guru Denise Duffield Thomas, when you have a negative thought about not being able to forgive someone or yourself, you need to say to yourself, 'I forgive you, I am sorry and I love you.' It may be hard to swallow initially, especially if you are thinking of someone who you feel has really wronged you. Her book 'Get Rich, Lucky Bitch' explains more for those of you who would like more explanation.

The exercise within this chapter is very powerful and if you use it regularly on issues you have with other people, you will find the negativity within you will disappear and you will feel lighter and brighter. Some memories can be really buried in our subconscious and can appear at any time. If you realise you have a problem with someone in your past or someone who is in your life now, then carry out the forgiveness ritual. It will make such a difference to you. I have recorded my own voice on my phone, so if I ever realise I need to forgive, I just listen to that. For a recording of the forgiveness ritual, go to: www.insightfulminds.co.uk.

You may just need to forgive yourself

The need for forgiveness may not just come from the need to forgive others. Regret is pointless. You can't change the past but you can change your future. You may be massively regretting some of your past actions and beliefs. You may be suffering from 'What if?' Whether you realise it or not, regret is a negative emotion. It makes you feel bad, which will make you feel heavier. The heavier you are emotionally, the harder it is to manifest the money you desire.

If you are feeling regret, then you are accessing past memories in your mind and again are not living in the present. You may be feeling guilty about money that you have spent that was not yours or in my case, that I had stolen. As a child, I felt poor and yes, I did steal money from my parents. I felt that I needed money to keep up with my best friend. She was being showered with money and gifts to remove the guilt her Mum felt for not being able to look after her full time while she worked.

I can't take back how I behaved, but I did learn from it. I was not being grateful for what I had at home i.e. being deeply loved and appreciated by my parents and family. I was well cared for and was well provided for. I carried around the guilt of stealing this money with me until only just a few years ago. It was a heavy weight.

Be non judgemental about others

It is really important to be non judgemental about others. I was judged a lot by people in business initially about my expertise in attracting money as I was honest about sharing that I was still in quite substantial debt. As a Reiki Master Teacher, I teach others to speak their truth and to be honest. Lying about what had happened did not help. I had 'acted as if' things were ok before and that got me into worse trouble! There were good reasons for why I had got myself into this dire financial situation.

I'd had significant bereavements which had led me into depression as well as being in a situation of not being able to discuss money openly with my husband. My number blindness led me to have problems as I was unable to calculate the figures behind my business which other people just took for granted. It wasn't about to turn around in a day. What people also didn't realise that I had been a healer for years and even when I was sick, I was healing others, so helping people with my skills whilst I worked on getting myself out of debt was the same principle!

I had feedback from networking friends telling me that they would not come on my money mindset courses as I was in debt and therefore not a great role model. I was being judged as I wasn't driving the flashiest and newest car. It was clear they were misunderstanding the money concepts I was teaching. I desperately needed their help to get myself out of the problems I had, but them judging me based on what I truthfully told them about my situation just did not help me. If they had referred people to work with me, I could have got out of debt and my depression crisis quicker.

I just wanted to use the skills and experience I had to help people and save lives, but wasn't able to easily find clients. What people around me did not realise was that my self worth energetically wasn't at a level to attract the work in and I was still having to reprogramme negative beliefs/patterns which came up which were blocking me.

I've had to 'act as if' I've not been in debt with the people around me and manage my money effectively to use the Law of Attraction to help me bring financial riches, even though I was spiritually very rich and grateful for everything I had in life.

Clearly I have forgiven my friends for acting as they have. Yes, they judged me, but also I know that I can take a while to trust people around me too and I was giving off a confused message about what I did. Hopefully this book will give them even more clarity. I did not realise that I was the Healer's Healer (my spiritual mission) and I did not make it easy for them to work with me or to refer their clients to me. They just did not know any better and unless they came on my money mindset workshops or tried out working with me on a 1-1 basis they never would! It was a catch 22 situation.

By forgiving myself and them for judging me, I am forgiving myself for judging them. Perception is projection after all. I have to take responsibility for my thoughts. I could be angry that they did not help me when I needed their help most, but it's the past. I take responsibility for my actions and for the debt that I found myself in. I created the problem and it was up to me to sort it out.

When you are with potential clients, be careful not to judge them about what money they do or don't have. How do you know if they can pay a lot or a little. Be transparent about your pricing with all your clients. If they value what you have to offer, they will pay. If you are thinking 'I wonder if they can afford my services?' then guess what, they will pick up on this. If you offer a great service to your clients, then you will attract in clients who are not concerned about price as they want to work with you.

Another thing others appeared to judge me for was that I was strong, capable and very experienced (which I am), so therefore I did not need help. They assumed I must have lots of work. I'm naturally a leader and I just take on this role. I give advice from my wisdom and experience and I have many contacts in business who help me understand more about what I need to do to make my business even more successful.

Just because someone is positive and kind, they may also have something else going on which is affecting their happiness. Always listen to another person and find out what is going on to get to know them. What most people didn't know is that I was verging on being suicidal about the debt I was in and I was very, very vulnerable.

Depression is a hidden killer and you never know how someone is being affected by it. Lots of people go up and down in business and this is normal as you are stepping out of your comfort zone but when significant things happen such as bereavements, relationship breakdown and chronic ill health, life can feel a lot harder. Often someone with depression will feel ashamed and will put on a brave front, when really they are struggling and need help but often because they are poor receivers, they will not ask for help and will suffer in silence.

I've met many business owners who have come from corporate and public sector employment who are depressed as they enter the business world. They have become so unhappy with their employment that they leave their jobs to set up a business. Without the right skills, experience and contacts in business, they then struggle to get their business off the ground, which then makes them feel worthless and lacking in vision and direction. They lose hope.

Exercise:

Practising a Forgiveness Ritual

It is important to let go of the negative emotion which you hold onto by being negative towards another person. It is not helping you. There is a Hawaiian forgiveness ritual called 'Ho' o Pono Pono (Making things right) which you can do. Google it to find out more information. There are various rituals which have been developed. Below is one which I have created. You can use it to forgive yourself and others.

If you hold onto negativity from a past relationship/friendship with someone, it is actually harming you and by letting go of this negative energy, you can allow yourself to feel lighter and brighter. By releasing this dark, negative energy, more lighter and brighter healing energy can return to you and you will feel more calm and relaxed about the person/people you have forgiven.

Forgiving yourself is the key to leading a happier life. Have no regrets, you have gone through these experiences for a reason and learn from them. Live in the present.

- ♥ *Sit quietly and bring to mind a person or people you need to forgive.*

- ♥ *Write down all the things where you feel that they have been negative towards you such as hurting your feelings or causing you fear and upset. Acknowledge to yourself that this negativity needs to stop and set an intention that today is the day for this to happen.*

- ♥ *Ask yourself what you need to learn from this situation so that it does not happen again. What are the blessings in disguise? (see pg. 137).*

❤ *Now as you sit quietly, visualise the person or people in your mind who you need to forgive. Remember any negative emotion you feel towards another such as anger, hate, fear or jealousy, is only causing you harm. You want to let go of the emotion to feel lighter and brighter about the situation and to help you to live in the present within your mind.*

❤ *See the person/people in your mind's eye and encase them in the white loving light of the Universe. Make the white light as bright as possible as if it is a beacon of positivity.*

❤ *Within your mind, visualise a loving and healing light coming down through the crown of your head, enlightening your whole body and allow the light to flow out of your body towards the person/people who are affecting you. Send them love and healing.*

❤ *Take this opportunity to speak up and to say what you need to say to them. Listen to what they need to say to you. Forgive them and thank them for what they have given you which you will have identified above as your blessings in disguise. Hear them forgive you for the unintentional harm you may have caused to them.*

❤ *When you have forgiven them, thank the person/people for what you have learnt. As you visualise this person/people in your mind, imagine that you are linked by a cord of white light. See in your mind, that you are holding a pair of shiny, silver scissors. Cut this cord of light with the scissors and see the cord of light return to the person/people you have in your mind. Allow all the positive energy to come back to you, now that you have released them. The person/people can now walk away from you and disappear for good. If you still see this person/people in the future, you will feel lighter and brighter and will no longer be triggered in the same way by them. Practising the forgiveness ritual is very powerful and can transform relationships and is especially useful if you are trying to heal a relationship and would like to repair it.*

♥ *You can record the forgiveness ritual and repeat it over and over again as new memories surface in your mind. You will find that each time you do it, it becomes easier and easier and you will feel more positive and connected with yourself.*

10

Are you a good giver and receiver?

'To give and not expect return, that is what
lies at the heart of love.'
Oscar Wilde

To ALLOW MONEY TO flow effectively in your life, you have to be both 'a giver' and 'a receiver'. What goes around, comes around. The problem is some people are so focussed on giving, that they just give too much and when they need to balance things up by receiving, they actually don't like it. This is how I was. I didn't feel worthy enough to receive what was on offer. A lot of people would much rather just be givers, but to have full health, wealth and happiness, you need to have a balance.

For example, how are you when you are offered a compliment about what you are wearing? Do you say 'thank you very much' or do you say 'what this old thing, I got it from the charity shop.' By giving and receiving you are opening up the flow of energy in life. What goes around, comes around. Just don't judge where something lovely is going to come from.

Are you open to receiving?

In one of my workshops, I give each participant a £1 coin to hold for an exercise. Later on in the session, I then give this £1 to the person. Some people say 'thank you very much' and others feel very uncomfortable or actually give it back to me even before I get a chance to give it to them. An abundant heart believes that if you give money, money will return to you. The money may not come exactly at that moment in time and abundance may come in the form of opportunities which earn you money or in the form of gifts.

If you are the sort of person who finds it difficult to receive a compliment or help from someone else, then there is work to do, as you need to be able to receive. An easy Louise Hay affirmation to say to yourself is 'I am open and receptive to all good.' You need to allow yourself to accept prosperity, whether that is time, love, success, joy, comfort, beauty, wisdom, good health or money.

I have been able to track the money made from all of my workshops. Once I openly gave £1 to all the participants to show the power of giving with an abundant heart. After the session, one of my current clients booked a session with me. This was worth £125. When I saw her for the session, I told her about getting good value Reiki sessions at pamper events and asked her if she wanted to come with me to an event. We went to this pamper event together and I had such a great conversation with a Reiki Practitioner there, that this lady booked a session immediately with me. Another £125! On the way home from the event, my current client said she wanted to become a Level 2 Reiki Practitioner with me. This was £400 more. As time went on, my new client from the pamper event referred her Mum to work with me, and I have so far earned £775 from giving my £1 away at the workshop. I had to be open to receive. Get the idea....

Another thing to be aware of is that when you are not having something you want, you are not allowing yourself to accept on some level. There is resistance in you. When you are truly open to receive, things are just given to you. What we give out, we get back and we have to be careful not to over take from someone. I teach people to accept what they are offered by just saying 'thank you very much' and without saying 'I will pay next time' or analysing who paid last time.

Now clearly if a friend is always paying, then you need to pay sometimes, but don't get hung up on rules of fairness! Also if something is offered to you that you just don't want or need, it is fine to say 'no thank you!' Just get into the habit of receiving compliments, great testimonials about your work as well as being offered free things such as tickets, room hire, business advice, etc. Just appreciate what you receive.

Do you notice how much you are receiving in life?

Everyday, we are given things in life from the people around us, but do we really notice everything we are given and are we grateful for what we receive? Life is so busy that you can just miss what you are given. We take life for granted and the people around us too if we are not careful. Life is a gift and just being able to breathe and function in life is something to be grateful for.

Pay attention to what you are receiving everyday. You may be given a discount for a book, or a free cup of coffee. These things have a value, but often we don't even notice and we are not grateful for what we are receiving. The more you give to others openly without anything in return, you will start receiving more in life including more money. Give without expectation of something for yourself though.

If you are adding up what a friend gives you and working out whether you have given enough, you are over complicating things. Remove any rules of 'fairness' in your mind i.e. you bought me this, so I have to buy you this to make it even! Look to spread happiness to others, without thinking about how it will help or benefit you. If you are thinking, but I don't have the money to give to someone else, then you are definitely living from scarcity now.

There are things you can give for free such as a smile, an item which you no longer want or need or just spending your time with someone can make a big difference. These all have a value. You can even donate blood or run a marathon for charity sponsored by others. If you are in debt, you don't give your 10% away to charity until you are debt free. Charity really does begin at home.

You may have heard about 'pay it forward' and wondered what this is about. You decide to perform random acts of kindness to unsuspecting people. This could be sending a book to someone, giving to the cashier the money for the shopping for the person behind you or just sending flowers randomly to a friend when there is no occasion. By spreading happiness this way, you will be passing on love to others.

In the excellent book 'The Go Giver', Bob Burg and John David Mann describes the 5 principles for success in life. These are:

- 💜 The Law of Value - Your true worth is determined by how much more you give in value than you take in payment.

- 💜 The Law of Compensation - Your income is determined by how many people you serve and how well you serve them.

- 💜 The Law of Influence - Your influence is determined by how abundantly you place other people's interests first.

- 💜 The Law of Authenticity - The most valuable gift you have to offer is yourself.

- 💜 The Law of Receptivity - The key to effective giving is to stay open to receiving.

You need to be giving to receive

As you can see you need to be giving to receive. The important thing is to be open to receive. There is no need to judge 'what' you are going to receive, just be ready to accept. Be giving to those around you without expecting payment to come from it. Ensure that you are serving lots of people. This might be by helping out a charity at a fun run or by managing a support group online which supports thousands of people. It has to be tailored to your own context. I know I have done free talks for support groups before and then a year later been booked to run a course for them, so the financial reward may not return for a while.

Focus on putting others interests first. Listen carefully to what others need or want and help them achieve their goals. By helping more people, more people will help you. The love game will be in action big time. Be authentic and honest with everyone around you and just pay attention to what you receive. Money will come to you in many ways and won't necessarily show up as physical cash. You might be given a discount off an item, or you may receive an opportunity to write for a magazine, that usually you would have to pay a lot of money to be featured in.

Allow the energy to flow from others to you and for you to pass on the energy/love to others. A continuous flow is what you are looking for as this shows true abundance and will only come from when you are looking after yourself and you are living from the feelings of joy and happiness. Your health is your wealth. If you over give and put other's happiness too much ahead of your own, then your health will suffer as you will resent not doing what you want.

For example, you are asked by your sister to take her out for tea, but what you already had planned was to go to Pilates. Putting your sister first once may be ok, but if this is a regular occurrence, it is showing a behaviour trait that you need to change. One thing to check is are you being selfless or are you just thinking about yourself? Putting others first (but not sabotaging your own happiness) is the key to having true success and happiness in life.

Exercise:

Do you track what you receive on a daily basis? By this I mean things given to you for free like lunch, a cup of coffee or a gift of some sort. You may have been given support or help by a friend. Start tracking it for a week and notice what you receive. Appreciating what you already have, will attract more money to you. How well do you track your money? One success strategy of wealthy people is that they track all their money on a daily basis. Are you doing this?

The power of positive thinking and affirmations

*'The more man meditates upon good thoughts,
the better will be his world and the world at large.'*
Confucius

I USED TO BE SUCH a negative person. I was just so sensitive to what other people said and took on board their worries too which weighed me down. I was very much a judger and perfectionist and this really impacted the opportunities which came my way. I was basically asking via the Law of Attraction to bring me bad things in life. The perfectionist in me made it worse as I never thought I was good enough as I was judging myself very harshly with my high standards. The ups and downs in my life have been overcome by me changing my thought processes, behaviour and becoming a much more positive person. Yes, challenges do still arise for me and life is not 'rosy' 24/7, but if it was, life would be boring wouldn't it?

Why is positive thinking needed?

You really have to be careful what you say to yourself and to not get swayed by others around you. If you are regularly walking into shops, looking at the tags and telling yourself 'I can't afford that', well guess what? You never will! Look at something in a shop that you desire, tell yourself that it is good value and work out what steps you need to undergo to make the purchase happen. What are the smaller steps to achieve the bigger goal? If you set a too bigger goal first, your mind will just tell you that it is not possible. For example, you might set yourself a goal to earn £1m by Christmas 2015. If you have only been earning £1000 a month until this point, then your mind will not be able to believe that you can suddenly earn £1m. Baby steps move you forward to your end goal. To ensure a goal happens, sometimes you need to pay some money towards it to make sure it happens. For example, paying a deposit for a holiday or booking a place on a course e.g. your end goal is to write a book, so by booking on the course, you are taking action towards your main goal.

Fear is a real problem. FEAR stands for – False Evidence Appearing Real. In the mind, there are 13 different thinking types according to Cognitive Behavioural Therapy (CBT). This is where a person may be thinking a thought 'Nobody likes me' and are making something more of a problem than it actually is. How do you know if someone likes you or not? You can't know definitely. Even if they don't like you, does it really matter?

Going to do your pitch when you first start networking can be terrifying, but only because we make it that way. We expect people to be judging us, which they are not. They are actually thinking, 'I remember when that was me' and are sympathising. Be intuitive and trust your gut feeling. This is when you are no longer procrastinating and overthinking everything and you have become a knower. You know that you are creating everything and therefore you know you can create anything you want to.

When you start realising that you are making a mountain out of a mole hill and start retraining your thinking to be positive and less scaremongering, you feel calmer. It is the same when you think about money. If you think, 'I can't make money from what I do', then you probably can't as you don't have enough belief in your product or service. If you don't have faith in your product and service, then you won't get many customers and therefore will make no money!

You must value your product or service for your business to survive. You may be acting too small in your mind about your business. Think and act big about your business. This means that you may need to project realistic growth in your business and you may be acting small as you are fearful of being big and being able to cope with the demands of a bigger business. Of course if you put in the preparation and structure, before it becomes too big, you will have no problem. Richard Branson created his Virgin group over years, and he has always thought on a large scale and globally in what he wanted to achieve. What are you thinking about your business? Are you thinking big or small?

According to the Secret app, 'Expectation is a very powerful attractive force, because it draws things to you.' As Bob Proctor (featured in the Secret film) says 'Desire connects you with the thing desired and expectation draws it into your life.' Expect the things you want, and don't expect the things that you don't want.

For example, are you expecting that you won't have any clients/customers during the summer months as it is the summer holidays or do you believe that you will get just as many clients/customers as any other time of year. Your desire to get work, linked with your belief that you will, is a winning combination. Of course you have to tell your clients that you are open during the summer holidays too and ensure you manage your finances well.

Often I will notice in my client's language that they are talking about 'life is a battle', well if they are thinking this, and acting it out, then of course, life will be harder and be a battle. If you are thinking something like this, then how about being more positive about life being easy and that you have calm and peace at all times. After all it is only you who is making life a drama!

When I am working with my clients about their relationship issues, a really common problem is that they are not positive about a good outcome in sorting out their communication issues. If you are having problems at home, it will undoubtedly affect your business and the results you are achieving.

If you are having difficulties with your partner, are you expecting them to have not done as you had asked? For example, you might have asked them to have cleaned up the house before you got home. You might be so used to them not following your requests, you expect them not to do it subconsciously. This is so common.

You get what you expect. Be positive and visualise things how you want them to be, rather than how you don't want them to be and notice the effect on your business and your personal life. When you are expecting someone not to do something, this is because you don't trust them to do it. So work on why you aren't trusting them and change this issue in you and notice the difference.

Trust is a very powerful emotion and when you are untrusting of those around you, this affects your feeling of being safe and secure and knowing that the Universe will provide you with anything you desire. I always work with all my clients on a 1-1 basis to resolve their anxiety and distrust issues as life is always so much more calmer and positive when they do.

The book called the 'One Minute Millionaire' by Mark Victor Hansen and Mark Allan says 'There are only two doors in life: the door marked 'Security' and the door marked 'Freedom'. If you choose the door marked 'Security', you lose both.' Security is linked to the past i.e. what you have known. Spiritual growth and achieving what you want will take you into the unknown and is marked 'Freedom'. If you are feeling insecure about money, then ask yourself, what is making you feel insecure. Is it something that someone else is saying or doing, which is causing you to feel insecure? If there is, change how you feel about it!

There may be a communication issue to sort out between yourself and a partner. Rather than ignoring it, speak to them. Listen to their point of view without butting in. Having this conversation may well be a part of your spiritual growth and is working on the belief 'I can't speak up' which I work a lot on with my clients. By thinking positively about something, and not 'expecting' something negative to happen, you can change your life completely, as the Law of Attraction will bring you what you desire.

The importance of a vision board and making it real

By having a vision board, you will be able to focus more on what you want to achieve in your life and business. A vision board is a pin board, with pictures on it which link to what you would like to manifest and experience in your life and business. In your mind you have a Reticular Activating System, which needs to see and then feel the items you desire to make them come into your reality. If you are not a naturally visual person like me, you have to fake it to make it happen by using a vision board.

As the Law of Attraction states to Ask, Believe and Receive and to take inspired action. You also need to be visioning in your mind the item or experience that you are wanting to achieve or create and seeing it as if you have it already. It is also important to feel deep gratitude and appreciation for the help and support you need to achieve it. If you find it difficult to see pictures in your mind, you may wish to do what I do. I feel as if I have the item or experience and imagine the happy feelings of success when I have it. I spin the feelings of happiness in my mind which makes it feel even more exciting and real. Have a go! I am getting better at visualising in my mind, but it is not one of my natural skills!

From a business perspective, you need a vision as to where your business is heading. This takes the form of a one page business plan (not the many page document with financial projections that you prepare to borrow money from the bank) which has your goals, strategies and actions in it. To ensure you achieve the best results, ensure that the life goals that you want to achieve through the success of your business are on your business plan.

For example, if you want to work three days per week to allow you to spend two days with your children, you need to plan for this and the finances around it and have the amount on your vision board and business plan. You need to have a further plan with your three year, five year and ten years goals on it too.

It is also really important to ensure that you have a joint vision with your partner and know what you are trying to achieve together. What are your joint dreams? How are you going to achieve them? This is so important, as often if only one of you is a business owner, the other partner can feel left out. They may not understand why their partner is away networking or working so hard, but if they understand why you are, and can see themselves included in the plans, then they will be more supportive of you and you can create success together.

A joint force gives much more stability to your business, will raise your 'positive vibe' and allows you to be working as a team towards creating the life that you desire together. Your relationship values will be more in alignment and you will feel so much happier which will give you more energy and stability.

What affirmations to use and when?

Affirmations are statements which you read to yourself or say out aloud regularly. They help set intent in achieving a new state, behaviour or object. In fact, everything you say in your head is an affirmation - positive and negative, which why it is so important to understand and pay attention to what you are actually saying to yourself. Jack Canfield and D.D.Watkins describe affirmations as being 'one of the most powerful ways to create a vibration match for what you want to attract into your life. The goal is to create positive, self affirming and self empowering statements that uplift and inspire you. There are two types of affirmations: positive affirmations and goal specific affirmations.'

Positive affirmations confirm and reinforce positive beliefs about yourself and others. Goal specific affirmations are designed to help you manifest specific things into your life.

Examples of a positive affirmation

'I am happy and abundant.'

'I create my life with joy and happiness.'

'I feel safe and secure.'

Examples of a goal specific affirmation

'I am oversubscribed for my NLP for Business workshops.'

'I am feeling wonderful on holiday in Spain, enjoying the sunshine on my face.'

'I am happily standing in my new home in the Kent countryside.'

For more information and detail about how to set specific affirmations, I suggest you read 'The Key to Living the Law of Attraction' by Jack Cranfield and D.D. Watkins.

I was at an exhibition recently and I met a holistic therapist called Emma Cook. I was chatting to her about my book and how affirmations can really make things happen in your life. She explained how she had recently created her business 'The Tranquility Room' www.thetranquilityroom.co.uk and had used positive affirmations to help her to set up her beauty room and business. She said she was amazed at the discounts she was receiving and the help she received in getting all the things she needed for the business. By using the affirmations, her business became more productive and within two days of going live, she was fully booked!

Her top daily affirmations are:

'My tranquility room is always busy.'

'I am a valuable person.'

'I am really good with money.'

'Money flows often and easily to me.'

'I am in control.'

'I am calm.'

'I can handle anything today brings.'

'I am always in the right place at the right time.'

'I am always presented with new opportunities to better myself.'

'Great things always happen around me.'

'My place of work is a harmonious place to work.'

'My client base is increasing fast.'

'I always have more than enough money.'

Why don't you try them out too. Make sure you are consistent though and say them every morning.

According to Mark Victor Hansen and Robert Allen in their fantastic book 'The One Minute Millionaire', the affirmation to say to yourself before you go to bed and as you wake up is

> *"I am abundant in every good way. Infinite money is mine to earn, save, invest and exponentially multiply and share. My abundance is making everyone better off. I embrace abundance and abundance embraces me."*

Whilst my book is written from a purely spiritual and non religious view point (each religion has its own set of beliefs), it is worth remembering that you are connecting to Source (i.e. whoever created you) when you are meditating. God to you could be a man or woman in the sky or basically anyone you think they could be. Some top affirmations to regularly say are: 'Thank God, I'm rich', 'I am enough' and 'I am loved, deeply loved.' By saying these regularly, you will be training your mind to have peace. Peace of mind is priceless.

I am a massive fan of Louise Hay who is a renowned global healer and thought leader. The four key elements Louise tells you to keep in your heart is being playful, joyous, feeling safe and peaceful. There are 12 affirmations I look at daily which are taken from Louise Hay's 2013 calendar.

'I now recognise my creativity and I honour it.'

'Love is all I need to fix my world.'

'I communicate with love and attract loving experiences and people to me.'

'I appreciate the beautiful world I live in.'

Exercise:

Take five minutes and look at the Louise Hay affirmations. Be honest with yourself. Which ones do you believe and which ones are you less sure of? What do you need to change in your behaviour to ensure that you truly believe and live the affirmations as if they are true?

'My thoughts weave the tapestry of my life.'

'I give myself permission to prosper.'

'I am always willing to take the next step.'

'I connect with the Power that created me.'

'I am in the rhythm and flow of an ever changing life.'

'My love and acceptance of others creates lasting friendships.'

'I bless others good fortune and know that there is plenty for all.'

'The love I give is the love that I receive.'

I regularly ask myself, am I being true to all of these affirmations? Do I really believe them? Do I need to change anything in my life to make the affirmations work? For example, it took me a while to accept and embrace that I was the Healer's Healer. It seemed like such a big responsibility and stepping up from the role I had been fulfilling so far. I have so much to teach other healers from my knowledge and experience and I now embrace this responsibility and know that this is the gift I have been given in life and by fulfilling my mission of spreading my knowledge and wisdom will heal many people through other healers.

But what happens if you are thinking, this is all very well, but it just isn't going to override the fact that 'I don't believe it is possible to change, that I don't feel in control and I don't feel good enough to carry on in business.' This is where learning the mindfulness techniques Emotional Freedom Technique, Neuro Linguistic Programming, meditation and self hypnosis would be really useful to you.

Energy and mindset technique for change

When I learnt how to use Emotional Freedom Technique (EFT), I was absolutely amazed about how it could transform both my energy and

163

thoughts. When I was depressed, the energy around me felt as if it was thick and I was walking through treacle. As I have said before, the winning combination to keep yourself well and healthy is medicine, mindset and energy and the beauty of using EFT is that you can overcome negative thoughts and reprogramme in positive thoughts as it is working on both your energy and mindset.

It is now commonly used by psychologists and within the mental health field. The best thing is, it is a technique anyone can use and it is free. It can be used to help you shift unwanted memories from the past, remove limiting beliefs, reduce pain and anxiety as well as having hidden benefits such as weight loss and giving you more energy. As you start removing the negative emotion from your body, linked to the negative experiences from the past, you will start to feel lighter and brighter.

EFT works by tapping on your meridian lines (energy points) in the body which link to your chakras. There is a particular sequence that you learn. The cause of all negative emotions is a disruption in the body's energy system. When we have a thought or memory from the past, it triggers a disruption in the body's energy system which is experienced as physical, psychological or emotional pain. The 11 negative core beliefs of 'I'm not good enough' discussed in Chapter 3 and the smaller limiting beliefs which link to them, are the key thought processes to work on when you are tapping on yourself.

When you are having a bad day and feeling that you can't move forward with your business, or you are doubting yourself, this is then the time to do EFT on yourself. In just minutes, you can transform yourself from feeling really nervous and tearful to feeling happy and positive. If you are procrastinating about doing something in your business which is affecting your success (and therefore your money), then use EFT on yourself. If you don't you will be sabotaging your success due to your own self worth issues.

EFT is a very practical skill and therefore not easily described within a book. There are specific points that you tap on your head, face and fingers, whilst saying a positive set up statement such as 'release stress', 'more energy' or 'I am in control'. I would recommend you use it when you notice yourself resisting change or if you are just not feeling on top form. It can very easily transform how you are feeling to become more positive.

EFT can reach great depths though and if you have had significant traumas in your life, I would suggest you work alongside myself or another therapist to manage this situation on a 1-1 basis. We can be holding onto very negative situations from the past in our minds and having someone guide you through understanding what you are experiencing is essential.

The basics of EFT are taught within some of my workshops. A video of the basics of using the 'Heart and Soul Protocol' developed by Sylvia Hartmann is available from my website, www.insightfulminds.co.uk. I teach all my clients how to tap, so that they have a quick self help technique, that can help them feel better fast. This can be used, just before you do your pitch, before a presentation or just when you wake up and you are feeling a bit overwhelmed. On a deeper level, it will help you feel more grounded and ready to deal with the challenges your business will throw at you.

Self hypnosis

Many people are really quite scared when the word 'hypnosis' is mentioned which is such a shame as it is so powerful. We talk to ourselves constantly and often very negatively and without compassion. Self hypnosis and/or going to see a hypnotist like myself for hypnosis are fantastic ways to transform how you are feeling, acting and believing quickly and with amazing results. When you are in a relaxed state, you can make really positive suggestions to yourself such as your affirmations and they will be more accepted by your subconscious mind and you will start to get really positive results.

According to http://www.wikihow.com/Perform-Self-Hypnosis, Self hypnosis is a naturally occurring state of mind which can be defined as a heightened state of focused concentration. By using it you can change your thinking, kick bad habits and take control of the person that you are - along with relaxation and destressing from daily life'. It is similar to meditation and results in a better you. Lots more information about how to hypnotise yourself is available online.

12

Insightful rituals
to embed positive money behaviour

'If you do what you have always done,
you will get what you have always gotten.'
Anthony Robbins

T O CREATE THE LIFE that you desire, you have to take a very honest and hard look at yourself and your behaviour. It does require some time and focus to go within and to ask yourself are there some things that you are doing in life that need to change? You have to develop positive habits to allow you to bring in more money into your life and to increase the flow of giving and receiving prosperity. This chapter gives you some ideas of rituals or habits to review, change and embed depending on how good or not you are already.

For example, if you are resisting tackling your accounts, don't track your mileage on a daily basis or you are happy living in a cluttered home and office, these would be habits to change to allow more flow of energy to come into your life. To learn or to change a habit, you have to change your current habit and behaviour at least 28 times to make it unconsciously competent. If you have lots to change, then the best way to tackle this, is to write down all the habits to change on a grid and track the fact that you have done it differently over 28 days. Over time, you will see that you are not consistent in some habits and you will be able to identify what to tweak and change. By making changes such as having a set time per week to carry out financial matters will allow you to feel more organised and controlled about your finances personally and in business. Successful people are consistent in their behaviour and rituals. To help identify some key money mindset behaviours/habits you might like to change, download the free money mindset tracker at www.insightfulminds.co.uk.

Top tips to gain happiness and abundance

It is time for you to manifest more in life. Manifesting is an art of changing something from your thoughts and bringing it into reality. These next steps will help you do this in a practical way.

1. You need to have a compelling 'why' you want it e.g. What will you do when you have more money? How will you use it and use it to help others?

2. Admit that you want more money. It is ok to desire it.

3. Say to yourself every day with real emotion and meaning 'I am rich, I am wealthy and I deserve it, and I love it'.

4. Clear your mind and meditate for just 5-10 minutes per day on abundance in your life. Practise self compassion every day.

5. Meditate on 'What can I do to bring more abundance into my life?' Clear the mind and allow stuff to come up, knowing that the issue will be resolved.

6. Appreciate what is abundant in your life right now. A few minutes after your meditation, express gratitude for what is going well in life.

7. Become a better receiver - let someone pay for you, let others help you and be consistent in your practises. Ask for help.

8. You can increase the effectiveness of visualisation by more than ten times, just by connecting with real emotions to what you are mentally imagining.

9. Visualise what you want to manifest, but attach a positive emotion to each image. How do you feel when you achieve it?

10. Some great affirmations to use:

   ❤ I live my life full of integrity and honesty

   ❤ I am an example of possibilities

   ❤ Life is a wonderful experience

   ❤ I have a supportive and uplifting circle of friends

   ❤ I inspire millions of people

   ❤ I live my life

   ❤ I travel the world

   ❤ I am positive and happy

   ❤ My life is abundant

Adapt your environment to make you feel good

A very cheap and easy way to clear your mind and to help you refocus on gaining more money personally and within your business is to clean, declutter, to decorate and to fix or throw away broken things. If you are living or working in an environment which is dirty, or really cluttered, it will subconsciously affect you, which will bring your vibe down and make you feel less happy. As you clean, decorate and declutter, you will feel more energised and focussed. Ensure you set goals to achieve at the same time as cleaning up and watch how quickly you can manifest more energy to achieve things in your business and life. Negative energy can get stuck and by 'cleansing' your environment this will help you move it on. Remember to give attention to your house, office, car and garden. Consider moving furniture around in your home and office too as this will make a difference. Be intuitive about where things should be.

You also need to declutter things such as your email system as if this is stuffed full with unread, unnecessary emails, it can make us feel overwhelmed and disorganised. One of the easiest ways to make more money quickly, is to choose your most cluttered room in your house and declutter and clean it. Often you discover things which you don't use and can sell and you will be removing aspects of your home which bother you subconsciously.

Ensure you review your garden space too and weed it regularly. If you have any high hedges which could be blocking the flow, then cut them down. Following my Mum dying, I remember looking at the walls surrounding my garden and realising that the ivy had grown at least a foot on top of it. Within an hour, all the ivy was removed and the house started to feel lighter as did I. Such a simple change, that made a big difference to me and it cost nothing.

So how well do you treat your car? Just like your house, your car represents your whole energy system. Is it covered in bumps and scratches? Do you respect it? Is it filled with crisp packets and old receipts? Is it clean inside and out? Professionally, people will judge you (rightly or wrongly) by your car and its cleanliness. If it looks a mess, this may well indicate to them that this is how you run your business, so they may not wish to work with you. This will of course affect you gaining custom and therefore the money you have.

In essence, value and appreciate your home, car, garden and office and you will notice a difference in how you are feeling and you will have more energy to help you in business. If you want to get the most out of this process, then declutter, clean and organise yourself around the lunar cycles at a New Moon and Full Moon. Spiritually, on a Full Moon you give up negative thinking patterns, things which are bothering you and on a New Moon, you set new goals and focus on what you are wanting to achieve to have the life and business you desire.

Be consistent

By being consistent everyday with all aspects of your life, you will find that the results you achieve will become more reliable and you will feel more stable. I do this by ensuring that all my habits are consistent and if I notice that I am going off track, I look at that behaviour within myself. Each evening, I have a set routine. I write down what I want to achieve the next day, I write in my gratitude journal about the positive aspects of my day and I look at my goals. I visualise the next day as the perfect day and ask for myself to be connected to all the right people. I then meditate for ten minutes and send love to myself, my network of friends and family and then out to the world.

The next morning as I wake up, I say to myself what I am grateful for, I visualise the perfect day and ask to be connected to all the right people to help them. I look at my goals. I then meditate for ten minutes again sending love to myself, my family and then out to the world. I do some stretches, drink some water with lemon as I go downstairs and I then always walk my dog Charlie to gain my exercise for the day. Are you being consistent with your habits?

Could you live life more frugally?

You may have lived a life where you could buy what you want, when you want or you might have lived a life where you just managed to pay the bills and if you had any money left over it was a bonus. The norm tends to be that people spend what they have and with the surge of credit, they have spent their income plus the credit that they have been given. Whilst I was employed, I was not in debt at all and all bills were paid on time. Whilst building a business, you have to start managing your money a very different way and train your mind to be comfortable with receiving money at different times rather than on a set date. Money does not arrive on set days as sometimes your clients just don't pay when they say they will and sometimes you have unexpected expenses to pay out for your business. You also have to invest in your business, especially at the start.

You have to start altering your behaviour around money in your personal life and your business. By looking at where you are shopping, how often you are shopping and following a smaller budget than you thought you could cope with, you will find that you will be able to afford more in the future. Often we buy stuff that we just don't need. By saving more money now, you can then invest in experiences which will give you lasting memories such as holidays, family moments and anything else adventurous you fancy doing. Appreciate every penny of money that you earn and change your behaviour around saving money, and enjoying it. Just by asking yourself on every purchase, 'Do I want or need this?' you will save thousands as you will realise how we buy needless items which have little value but cost us money.

According to some recent research by Aviva (www.thisismoney.co.uk), Brits spend nearly a thousand pounds on 'invisible' small items like tea, coffee, snacks, cigarettes and shop-bought lunches every year on average. People spend £18.23 each week on 'invisible' goods, adding up to £947.96 a year on average. Over a person's lifetime, this could stack up to roughly £47,398 per person, Aviva reveals. By cutting back on these items, people could build up an average pension pot of around £136,000, the findings suggest.

As a small business owner, it is easy to spend money every day buying coffees, water, lunches for business contacts and just because they are busy, money is not saved where it can be. By being more organised, you can bring your own water to meetings or a coffee in a mug to go to save money as well as planning and cooking meals ahead at home which you can pull out of the freezer. Batch cooking items from fresh and freezing ready for when you need them, means even more money can be saved and it is healthier for you too.

Shopping in a lower priced supermarket can save you thousands of pounds. Even if you just buy your basics from these supermarkets or discount shops, you will save money. The key is to put your head into 'frugal mode' by thinking to yourself on each purchase 'How can I save money?' This builds up a new respect for money. Ask for discounts on items and buy sensibly. Sometimes you can get great deals online as well. Ask people in your network for advice about how to save money on things before you purchase too. Other business people are always keen to show you how to do something economically as they know how expensive it can be from being in business.

When you were not a business owner, you lived life at as a consumer. You just bought from businesses whether it be clothes, food, double glazing, landscape gardening or a massage, without considering that the business owner had to pay out for their personal expenses, their business expenses and make a profit too. As a business owner, you have to pay for personal development, advertising, marketing, accountancy, websites, networking, training and more and it is really expensive being in business. Being frugal and looking for discounts will help you achieve your dreams, even if it isn't your usual way of life at the moment.

There are other ways to save money too. You can go to free networks which run every day. The key is to go regularly, and to help as many people as possible and look for collaborations which could help your business. Working with others rather than trying to do everything yourself will save you money. There is free training on offer which you can participate in online and offline until you have money to invest. It is best to try to run your business without credit or loans first, even if you have to have a part time job initially to pay for your personal expenses which will make you feel more secure. Shopping around for a good deal for all your personal bills and business expenses is a necessity too.

You may be surprised by the response of your utility providers if you say you are leaving them. When my husband left, I had to look at all expenses in my house. To be honest, I hadn't given them enough attention. I was paying £25 per month to have Sky tv. Clearly it is not a necessity when your mortgage needs to be paid. I had gone over the 12 month contract and therefore I had Freeview installed. I asked Sky to stop my contract and they immediately offered me a deal of £10 per month as I had been a loyal customer for ten years. I still decided to cancel completely and to be honest, I don't miss watching tv now.

If you are in significant debt, and you are feeling out of control and find it difficult to change this, you may need to consider getting a full time position to pay the bills initially, to rebuild your self worth and to allow you to feel more secure. This potentially could mean putting your business on hold for a period of time. Only you can decide if this is the right course of action.

Whilst this could be seen as a scarcity mindset, your mental health is more important and getting in cash quickly to start paying bills and feeling stable would allow you to refocus on your business and look at how you can change it in the future when your funds are more abundant.

As mentioned before, live within your means and only give to charity after you are out of debt. When you are not in debt, you can start giving away 10% of your income, save 10%, spend 10% on yourself and allocate the other 70% on paying your bills and tax. If you have anything left, look towards saving it.

Remember to set goals

When it comes to setting goals, remember that clarity is power. It is essential that you have a one page business plan which links to your vision board. You need to have goals and ensure your goals are SMART. Specific, Measurable, Achievable, Relevant and Timely. You don't want to think of your goals, but think from your goals. See your goals in your mind's eye and

Exercise:

If you were being really honest now, how do you think you waste money? What items could you downgrade or save money on right now? How can you shop more conservatively?

visualise them as if they have been achieved. Feel gratitude for all the good fortune you are having in reaching them including any help you are receiving. It is important to write your six main goals down every day, to help you stay on track.

This will help you make choices when opportunities come your way. Sometimes it is necessary to pass up on opportunities as you can see the bigger picture for your business which in the long run will make you more money. Be abundant and give those opportunities to someone else who could benefit. Visualising your goals as if they are achieved each evening and morning before you meditate will help you create your vision faster. It is essential that you set financial goals for your business and you have done the ground work to see what you need to achieve to be able to earn the amount of money you are projecting.

When it comes to goals, think big! If you have struggled to make money in your business, you probably have not been stretching yourself enough. When I was really struggling, I was grateful for any money which came in, no matter how small it was, but I was working without a concrete vision or with targets which would make it a reality. Clearly you have to initially work within your means, but remember that a small business with focus, will grow and eventually can and will be one of those big corporate companies if you wish.

Gratitude

I can't stress enough how important it is to focus on gratitude every day and on a regular basis throughout the day as it will improve your vibe. In the morning, say your ten gratitudes and intend a great day.

Using some of the techniques I have learnt from 'The Magic' by Rhonda Bryne, I expect things to happen by intentionally applying gratitude. Go for something small first such as a parking space and then go for bigger stuff over time as it has to go in alignment with you believing something is possible. All you have to do is say in your mind 'Thank you, thank you, thank you for my parking space.' and visualise the space you desire and act as if you are going to receive it. I always get a parking space whenever I want one even if the car park is really busy!

Now start to apply the act of saying 'Thank you, thank you, thank you...' before anything you are desiring and feel a sense of gratitude that your wish will be fulfilled and let go of the outcome. As mentioned before, when you ask for what you desire, believe it is possible and take inspired action, you will receive it. If it is not working for you, then you may well have a problem with your beliefs or are not truly willing to receive as you have to be in flow to receive what you are asking for.

At the end of your day, go through your day in your mind and reflect on all the good things that have happened, no matter how small. If you have had a bad day, then try to see the blessings in disguise i.e. what did you learn from the situation that you are grateful for? This will help you stop repeating patterns in your life.

How much money do you want to earn?

We can get so wrapped up in having our business that we can lose sight of just how important the numbers are in our business, especially if we don't like numbers or our maths ability is poor. If it is not your thing, buddy up with someone who does it well and workout the figures. Have you decided what your vision is for this year, next year, three years, five years and ten years and what financial targets you want to meet? If you haven't written down some statistics for your business, how are you going to track your progress? Link these figures to your vision board and one page business plan and let the magic take place.

Have you set an intention of how much money you want to earn and by when? Holding a vision of what you would do with money rather than focusing on money itself, is a more effective way of attracting money in.

When you have worked out how much you want to earn, you can then work out what steps you need to take to get it. Yes, you might have to move deadlines a bit as things happen in life, but if you are working to a plan, you will find that you will be more on course to succeed and to make the money you desire in your business. Remember to include numbers linked to your website audience, people attending your events and be specific about how many customers you want. Use the money manifestation techniques below to gain the money you desire.

Tracking your money and what you receive

It might sound boring, but you need to start tracking the money that you receive and spend each day. You need to make it a habit to know when payments are coming out of your accounts and what money is in your accounts too. This is a behaviour taken from millionaire entrepreneurs and it really is your choice whether you adopt this technique or not, but it would be my strong advice to you to do it. This will help you eliminate money leaks in your personal and business expenses and will enable you to feel more in control of your money.

By having this control, you will find you are respecting money more and this in turn will allow you to grow the money that you have to invest in your business as well as living the life you desire. You will also find it helps to have a set time to focus on your finances especially if it is not your favourite job.

As mentioned before, another habit is to record what you receive each day from other people and to express gratitude. Sometimes we are so busy, we just don't notice what we are given. For example, it could be a free pen you receive from a conference (remember there are countries out there where kids are desperate for pens to write with) or it could be a cup of coffee or dinner that your friend bought for you.

Exercise:

What can you do to change the amount of money you have? If you are being honest with yourself, what habits do you need to change?

The money manifestation technique

According to Napoleon Hill's 'Think and Grow Rich' book which was written in 1937, there is a six step process to take to gain the money you require. Clearly this technique is to summon up an exact amount, rather than creating projections for your business, although it can work in the same way.

- Fix in your mind the exact amount of money you desire. It is not merely enough to say 'I want plenty of money'. Be definite about the amount.

- Determine exactly what you intend to give in return for the money you desire (There is no such reality as 'something for nothing'.)

- Establish a definite date when you intend to possess the money you desire.

- Create a definite plan for carrying out your desire and begin at once, whether you are ready or not, to put this plan into action.

- Write out a clear, concise statement of the amount of money you intend to acquire, name the time limit for its acquisition, state what you intend to give in return for the money, and describe clearly the plan through which you intend to accumulate it.

- Read your written statement aloud, twice daily, once just before retiring at night and once after arising in the morning. As you read, see and feel and believe yourself in the possession of the money.

- It is important that you follow the instructions described in these six steps. It is especially important that you observe and follow the instructions in the sixth paragraph. You may complain that it is impossible for you to 'see yourself in possession of money' before you actually have it. Here is where a burning desire will come to your aid. If you truly desire money so clearly that your desire is an obsession, you will have no difficulty in convincing yourself that you will have it.

Only those who become 'money conscious' ever accumulate great riches. 'Money consciousness' means that the mind has become so saturated with the desire for money, that one can see oneself already in the possession of it.

Remember that money is not the root of all evil and it is not greedy to want it. You need money in your business to help all those customers you want to serve. Business costs must be covered and if you are struggling for money, you will not be able to serve your customers effectively.

Six principles to create the life you want

One of my trainers Lindsey Agness from the Change Corporation says there are six principles you need to follow to create the life that you want.

Principle No.1. Get clear on your goal

Think about something important that you want to achieve over the next twelve months. What really motivates you? Now check that goal is specific, measurable and timed. Focus on your goal. Whatever you put your attention on in your life will grow stronger.

Principle No.2. Know why it is a must

What are your reasons for wanting to achieve your goal? Ask yourself, 'If I don't do this now what will it ultimately cost me?'

Principle No 3. Take massive action

Are you prepared to do whatever it takes to achieve your goal including things that you do not want to do? Think right now of one small step and one large step you can take today and begin to move forward towards your goal. Challenge yourself by asking if you are taking personal and 100% responsibility for your goal. Because, to the extent that you do not, you are giving your personal power away.

Principle No 4. Know what you are getting

Be very aware of what works and what doesn't. Ask for feedback and constantly evaluate your approach. Think of feedback as a gift and remember to learn from any action that does not quite go to plan.

Principle No 5. Be prepared to change your approach

There is a saying 'if you always do what you've always done, you'll always get what you have always got!' You must be prepared to be flexible to move into the unknown. Security is an attachment to the known and the known is our past. No evolution in that. When you experience uncertainty you are on the right track - if you become too fixated on how to achieve your goal you shut out a whole range of possibilities.

Principle No 6. Ask for help from those who are already successful

When making major life changes, the most successful people in life are those who have already 'done it'. They do this by going on courses, being coached or simply asking for advice. You will probably find that with the appropriate support you will find the process of change more enjoyable and your chances of success will be greatly increased.

The power of meditation

Meditation is key to your success in achieving the money you require, whether that is to get out of debt or just to achieve your dreams. Meditation will allow you to discover the inner you, reconnect yourself with your higher self and the interconnectedness of mind, body and spirit. Meditation should be done twice a day if possible for at least ten minutes. To be most effective, you should meditate in the 30 minutes before going to sleep and in the 30 minutes as you wake up as your brain is in the alpha state. It is based on Eastern philosophies and has been around for generations.

According to Bev James of the Coaching Academy and Entrepreneur's Business Academy, Google have just put 1000 of their staff through company sponsored mindfulness meditation training to enable them to tap into creativity, become more focussed, to become better leaders and to ditch stress. Facebook have added a meditation room to their headquarters. So if big business is getting involved and you want your small business to become big one day, then meditation is essential to your success.

How to meditate

Your breathing is key to effective meditation. Consciously, breathe in positivity through your nose and negativity through your mouth. There is no need to sit in a lotus position or to have crossed legs. You can sit in a chair or lie down. It is your choice as both will work. The most important thing is that you are comfortable and can be quiet for a period of time as you want to be able to empty your mind effectively. If you are sitting, make sure your back is supported and your legs are not crossed which will allow the energy to flow more in your body.

Before you meditate, you may decide to ask yourself a question to get a response to something you have been struggling with. Whilst meditating, it is really effective to think of other people you know and don't know and send them love and compassion. You might start with giving yourself love, then widening it out to people in your family, friends, and networking acquaintances and then sending even more out to the world, especially to areas which you know are in need e.g. disaster areas, war zones, etc. Remember sending worry to another person is not empowering them, which is why positive vibes need to be sent out at all times. It is also very powerful to send love and compassion to those people in your life who are causing you problems. As with the forgiveness ritual in Chapter 9, you will create a positive result for yourself.

If you are going to ask yourself a question before meditating, according to Ed Lester, an abundance coach, say to yourself 'I am going to attract wealth. It will happen. Please share some ideas and direction for how we are going to make this happen?' rather than saying 'I need to make money fast.' By giving yourself more direction, you will allow your mind to be directed to find the solution for you.

You can find a recording of the 'healing tree' meditation at www.insightfulminds.co.uk. To learn more about guided meditation like the healing tree or mindfulness meditation, you will find details about the mindfulness coaching and training I offer on my website. I deliver 1-1 and group sessions.

Visit the healing tree for guidance and healing

1. Ensure you are in a quiet environment, where you are not going to be disturbed for 15 minutes. You need to make sure that you are warm enough, as your body temperature will go down as you relax.

2. What do you want to learn about yourself today by meditating? Set your intention before you close your eyes. You might want to ask yourself a question to gain guidance on how to proceed with something in your life, or you might just want to allow your subconscious to reveal what it wants you to learn. Either is fine. By doing this, your unconscious will help you to become aware of the answer to specific questions or will show you images that will help you generally in understanding how to move forward in your life.

3. Sit on a straight backed chair and uncross your legs. This allows the energy to flow through you easily and helps you to clear your mind. It opens up the chakra system and the channel of energy which flows through your spine, which allows you to bring down higher vibrational energies from the spiritual universe into this world. Close your eyes and take a deep breath, and let it out through the mouth. Allow your body to relax in this position. Let your arms rest gently in your lap and your legs to relax into the floor.

4. Take two more deep breaths in through your nose (bringing in positivity) and exhale (negativity) through the mouth. As you breath out, feel any tension drop out of your body. In fact, you may like to say to yourself 'As I breath out, I allow all my worries and problems to melt away. I am deeply relaxed.' You will feel your eyelids becoming heavy. You can open and close your eyes and ask yourself to go further into deeper relaxation.

5. Now imagine that you are walking along a country path. It is a beautiful day and the path is lined with trees which are swaying in the wind. The sun is beating down and you are feeling loved and enlightened. As you

walk along the path, you can feel the stones underneath your feet and you notice the different colours of the leaves which are blowing in the wind. They are multi coloured - reds, greens, browns, yellows, gold. As you see the leaves floating down you feel deeper and deeper relaxed in your chair. You feel at peace with yourself.

6. As you walk along the path, you come across a purple door with your name engraved on it in golden italic lettering. You are curious about what is on the other side of the door. You decide that it is time to take the plunge and to see what is there. Using the golden door handle, you walk through to find yourself in a beautiful bluebell wood.

7. It is the most stunning wood you have ever been in. You are surrounded by magnificent strong and magical trees. You are in awe of the deep purple of the bluebells and as you walk along the path, you can feel the bark underneath your feet. You feel a deep sense of peace and relaxation as you breathe in the scent of the bluebells and devour the beautiful view in front of you.

8. As you walk forwards you notice how many animals are living in harmony together in the wood. You notice squirrels, foxes, mice, deer, badgers and lots more and you are entranced by the multi-coloured butterflies which are floating up, and up and up and down and down and down with the wind. You are feeling even more deeply relaxed. The birds are tweeting and you are feeling on top of the world and a deep sense of peace and calm inside. As you walk through the woods, you come across a wooden staircase going down a slope. You have no idea where this is leading to, but your inner wisdom is indicating that it is safe to go there.

9. There are ten steps down and you are currently on step 10. As you step down each step, unload any anxieties or worries that you have been holding onto and leave them on the step. Step 9....Step 8.....Step 7.... Feeling more and more relaxed....Step 6, Step 5, Step 4....feeling deeper

and deeper relaxed. Step 3, Step 2, more and more relaxed, Step 1.... and you find yourself in a beautiful country meadow. What a stunning place. As you wander through the long grasses, the sun still beating down, you are just at one with nature. You can see a big oak tree in the distance and you walk towards it. This is the healing tree. As you walk through the meadow, you notice all the beautiful flowers, daisies, buttercups, poppies. A riot of colour. You can feel the long grasses against your legs as you walk towards the tree.

10. You come across a trickling stream with stepping stones over it. Before you cross, look into the water, see your reflection and throw any negativity you may be holding onto into the water and see it washed away. Send the negativity further and further away, seeing it getting smaller and smaller until it is just a speck on the horizon.

11. Now walk across the stream and head towards the tree. It is beckoning you. As you approach the Healing Tree, you notice that there is a beautiful, engraved wooden seat underneath it. You take a seat. The tree has some wisdom for you. You have been ignoring guidance being given to you and now is the time to listen. Relax and take note of what you are being told. Once you have taken note, spend some time here sending loving and kind thoughts to yourself, your friends and family and out to the world.

12. Remain in this place for five minutes or so (extend in the future when more practised).

13. When you want to come out, just retrace your steps. Go up each step of the staircase from 1- 10 feeling lighter and brighter with every step. When you reach the 9th step, feel the energy beginning to return to your body. As you reach the 10th step, take a big deep breath. Open your eyes and slowly bring yourself up to conscious awareness, feeling the energy return to your legs and arms and eyes and mouth and head and neck. Feel your breathing return to normal. Wake up easily, open your eyes and when you are ready, you can get up.

Notes:

Notes:

Notes:

Notes:

Notes:

Notes:

Notes:

Checklist to help you stay on track

Daily reminders

♥ Visualise your day how you want it every day in the morning & evening ☐

♥ Look at your vision board every day and update it with new images regularly ☐

♥ Use the money tracker to ensure your habits become unconscious competent ☐

♥ Use the Healing Tree meditation or another form of meditation twice daily ☐

♥ Maintain a daily focus on what is important to you ☐

♥ Say to yourself at least ten things that you are grateful for today ☐

♥ Look at your six main goals in the morning and evening ☐

♥ Ensure you do at least 20 minutes of exercise ☐

Being attractive to the Universe

♥ Love, respect and accept yourself ☐

♥ Take time for yourself and to relax ☐

♥ Enjoy what you do ☐

♥ Be naturally generous ☐

♥ Be happy and positive most of the time ☐

♥ Share your happiness with others ☐

♥ Take responsibility and ensure your language is positive ☐

♥ Compliment others and receive compliments easily ☐

♥ Believe in yourself ☐

♥ Relax regularly to let go of negative thoughts and to clear your mind ☐

Specific money behaviours

♥ You respect money by spending it wisely ☐

♥ You value what you offer in return for money ☐

♥ You respect money by knowing how much you have. Track debt too ☐

♥ You can comfortably talk about money without feeling anxious ☐

♥ You are tracking your money on a daily basis and what you receive ☐

♥ You sleep well at night knowing that you are financially secure ☐

♥ You make a clear intention when you want something ☐

♥ You have clarity of what you desire in the future ☐

♥ You stay on top of your clutter - in your home, office, car and garden ☐

♥ You focus on helping others and serving them ☐

♥ You appreciate the riches already in your life - friends, family, home, nature ☐

♥ You love being inspired and taking action ☐

♥ You take regular holidays and cut off from technology fully ☐

♥ You are eating healthily every day and drinking at least eight glasses of water ☐

♥ You are exercising at least 20 minutes a day ☐

♥ You enjoy a healthy work/life balance ☐

Reference books and resources
(Borrow books from the library or friends if you are in debt!)

How to become a Money Magnet in 21 days by Marie Claire Carlyle

Change your life with NLP by Lindsey Agness

The Secret by Rhonda Byrne

The Magic by Rhonda Byrne

I can do it by Louise Hay

Heal your life by Louise Hay

The Go Giver by Bob Burg and John David Mann

The Go Giver Sells More by Bob Burg and John David Mann

Acres of Diamonds by Russell Conwell

You can have what you want by Michael Neill

Think and Grow Rich by Napoleon Hill

Get Rich, Lucky Bitch by Denise Duffield Thomas

The Wealth Chef by Ann Wilson

Money - Master the Game by Anthony Robbins

Money and the Law of Attraction by Ester and Jerry Hicks

The Answer - Supercharge the Law of Attraction and find the secret to true happiness by Glenn Harrold

The Key to Living the Law of Attraction by Jack Canfield and D.D. Watkins

Change your questions, change your life by Marilee Adams

Become a Key Person of Influence by Daniel Priestley

Energy EFT by Sylvia Hartmann

The One Minute Millionaire by Mark Victor Hansen and Robert Allan

Is Your Life Mapped Out? by Dr David Hamilton

Mindfulness - A practical guide to finding peace in a frantic world by Mark Williams and Danny Penman

Ask and It is Given by Esther and Jerry Hicks

Stuff for Business by Ash Lawrence

Delegate to Elevate - 7 Steps to Success for Sole Traders by Sally Marshall

Email newsletter (4th October 2015) by Sunil Bali

Tweet @KentLifeCoach (13th October 2015) by Caroline Hart

www.core-beliefs-balance.com/example_negative_core_beliefs.htm

www.thisismoney.co.uk/money/pensions/article-3289670/Swapping-coffees-snacks-pension-pot-money-help-build-136k-nest-time-retire.html#ixzz3pr0gq5AP

www.the-coaching-academy.com/blog/coaching-articles/could_mindfulness_be_the_key_to_success.html by Bev James

www.wikihow.com/Perform-Self-Hypnosis [Accessed on 8/11/15]

Resources

The Magic Cheque - www.secret.tv

The Secret app - A day by day reminder of hints and tips to get the LoA to work

Practitioner & Master Practitioner of NLP notes by David Shepherd and Tad James

Believe and Achieve - A collection of inspirational thoughts and images

The Shift Film with Dr Wayne Dyer

Inspirational tips from Emma Cook www.thetranquilityroom.co.uk

Information about the Author

Liz Almond lives in rural Maidstone with her dog Charlie and cat Poppy. She is an inspirational Spiritual Teacher, Therapist, Coach and Business Mentor, who has spent her life learning how to help others. Liz had an accident in 1996 which was a catalyst for change. It led to her having two years off work and looking for answers about how to regain her health. Positivity and overcoming adversity have been the theme through her life and Liz has recovered her health dramatically.

When she started her business, she was confronted with a run of personal bereavements leading her into depression which affected her success, and her business floundered. She found herself in significant debt and had to apply different techniques to regain her wealth. She uses a heart centred approach to get the best for her clients and to help them learn by not making the mistakes she made in life.

Liz runs a multi award winning business. She has won the Bronze Award - Alternative Practitioner of the Year at the Kent Health and Beauty Awards 2015 as well as being a finalist for Coach of the Year 2016 and Specialist Coach of the Year 2015 with the Association of Professional Coaches, Trainers and Consultants. She also won the Kent Independent Trader Award for Health and Beauty two years running.